Summer Wine

with Jenny Haskins

A Quilt by Jenny and Simon Haskins

Quilters' Resource®

First published in USA in 2007
by Quilters' Resource Inc
Phone: Toll Free 1800 676 6543
Email: info@quiltersresource.com

Text: Jenny Haskins
Quilt by: Jenny and Simon Haskins
Designer: Suzy King
Photography: Tom Evangelidis
Styling: Jenny Haskins and Robyn Wilson

National Library of Congress
Cataloguing-in-Publication Data applied for
Haskins, Jenny
Haskins, Simon
Summer Wine
ISBN 1 – 889682 – 55 – 1(pbk.).

Printed in China

Summer & Wine

with Jenny Haskins

A Quilt by
Jenny and Simon
Haskins

From the Cellar Door

SIMON AND I ARE SO EXCITED TO BE PRESENTING *SUMMER WINE* – a quilt of extravagance, luxury and total decadence. The designs have been modified from those on our *Bella Fiori* design CD and then combined to make this gorgeous quilt. All are included on the *Summer Wine* design CD that is included with this book, proudly sponsored by Bernina.

Simon, for those of you who do not already know, is my son and business partner. He is an accomplished published artist in his own right – his *Aquamarine Ambience* was published by Quilters' Resource and *Simon's Folly* and *Moulin Rouge* were both published by Pride Publishing. Simon has traveled the world with me, teaching at such prestigious shows and exhibitions as the *IQA Markets and Festivals, Bernina University* (along with other sewing machine conventions), the *Martha Pullen Schools* and numerous other sewing and quilting shows and dealers' stores across the US.

The original designs on the *Bella Fiori* design CD were inspired by an antique, hand-embroidered Italian velvet altarpiece that originated in Rome. I divided the embroidery design into sections to fit a large hoop, then painstakingly sketched each section, adding my own personal twist to each design. You can see how the designs went together in *Creative Expressions* No 8, which replicates their combination on a gloriously embroidered black velvet shawl, trimmed with a 24in antique silk fringe that originated in China.

Summer Wine grew over a period of time. Simon and I began with a concept in our heads that we then created on the computer using design software; the designs were then combined and modified to suit our concept. At first we were going to put it together as a whole cloth quilt, but as it progressed we instead saw the quilt with a center medallion surrounded by elaborately embroidered wide borders rather than sashed blocks.

Simon, Robyn and I spent many rewarding hours embroidering and piecing the *Summer Wine* quilt. We actually pieced the quilt while Simon was in Bangladesh, visiting a friend who is working with street children there. Cell phone cameras really are wonderful devices! I rang Simon when the quilt was finished and told him the good news, and he said to send him a photo. I took the picture with my phone and he had it within 10 minutes – ain't technology grand!

Our wonderful Kim Bradley (you will be seeing more of Kim's amazing quilts) helped me quilt a good part of *Summer Wine*. My time had simply run out and Kim performed her usual magic. Kim had also quilted *Moulin Rouge* for us, which is just amazing.

The beauty of the *Summer Wine* designs is not only that they can be made into this glorious quilt, but that the individual sections of the quilt are equally beautiful made into pillows, pillow shams, tablerunners, wall-hangings and items of clothing – the list is endless (and so too are the number of possible color combinations; see pages 16–19). We have also used the designs as easy *Embroidery Decoupage* on furniture, mirrors, a foot warmer for the bed and matching pillow shams in delightful spring colors of pink and lime green.

Making the *Summer Wine* quilt presents an exciting challenge, and when it is finished the feeling of accomplishment will be amazing. The best thing about making this quilt, however, is your personal 'coming of age'.

So come with us as you discover your own *Summer Wine* – enjoy its color and bouquet, reminiscent of the fine wines served on the tables of a Tuscan villa.

Join us at our table, and sip on our *Summer Wine* while you enjoy the process of grape picking, blending and sitting back as you watch your *Summer Wine* mature 'grapefully'.

Ciao!

Summer Wine
Contents

As the song from The Sound of Music goes …
These are a few of my favorite things:
crisp sheets just in from a sunlit line,
morning light streaming in my bedroom window to awaken me,
and an original quilt to comfort me as I rest.

What could be more perfect than our *Summer Wine* quilt made with the friends and family we love? In my case, Simon (my son and right hand) and Robyn (my friend and the calming influence in my life) are the ones who are most responsibie for the embroidery; they spent countless hours cutting, changing threads and perfecting the art of accurate placement – what an amazing pair. Of course Simon is also our graphic designer on the computer, and was busy compiling the designs in sequence until we were both happy with the end result. The construction and quilting were left to me and Rob (Simon was off gallivanting overseas!) and, when time ran out for the quilting, Kim Bradley came to the rescue. Thank you to everyone – together you are an amazing team.

More than any other room in a house, the bedroom is the room in which we dream and renew our energies, where we can melt beneath the covers of our *Summer Wine* quilt. The bedroom meets our most essential needs as we retreat to it, gently closing out the world at the end of a long day.

My bedroom is my sanctuary and shelter; it is where I spend one-third of my life, renewing the intimacies of romance, and it is where the fond memories of snuggling my three infant children come from. At the end of each day, my bedroom beckons me – it is a place of softness and warmth, where I close the door on the day just past and open my eyes to each new morn. How beautiful is it to welcome each day from under the covers of our *Summer Wine* quilt.

Cellar Master's winning formula
tips, tricks & techniques

THESE TIPS ARE GUARANTEED TO GIVE THE NOVICE EMBROIDERER
perfect results every time, and to teach the more experienced artist how
to embroider a quilt with even greater ease.

So take the time to read and understand this section carefully, as it promises a *smooth tasting wine* when you reach the embroidery and construction stages. Considerable preparation is involved in cutting, printing and combining the templates, and preparing and marking the fabric pieces to be embroidered, so allow yourself uninterrupted time and an uncluttered space with plenty of light to avoid frustration and ensure accuracy.

DESIGNS AND TEMPLATES

Designs

1   There are 20 multi-formatted designs on the *Summer Wine* CD that accompanies this book. Use the Bernina design software *Version 5* and transfer device to transfer these embroidery designs from the design CD to your computer and then to your machine. It is best to transfer the designs on a need-to-use basis. Please note that **sw20** is not used in the quilt; it is a bonus design for you to play with.

2   To get a basting stitch to suit your hoop size, go to the Bernina website (www.berninausa.com), select **What's New** and then select FREE Downloads. Select Free Embroidery Hoop Basting Designs, then the appropriate hoop size for your machine, and then download this to your computer. (*Summer Wine* designs use the 255mm x 145mm oval hoop.) Follow the directions on the website for the use of basting stitch in conjunction with your embroidery designs. This basting stitch should be placed around all your embroidery designs.

3   All the designs here use the same Robison-Anton thread colors and numbers that we used in the *Summer Wine* quilt. These threads are available in the *Summer Wine* thread collection boxes.

4   To get the most out of your machine, remember to clean and oil it, and change your needle, regularly – it is uneconomical not to.

Templates

5   Use the Bernina Embroidery software, a PC and a regular printer to print placement templates on vellum tracing paper for all of the embroidery designs.

6   Use an awl to punch holes on each end of the vertical and horizontal divide lines that intersect the center of the design, and also through the center on each vellum placement template.

7   The placement holes you have punched in each template are used when the template is positioned (in the desired place) over the fabric. A fabric-marking pen is then used to mark a dot through the punched holes onto the fabric. The dots are then connected using a quilter's ruler and fabric-marking pen, thus replicating the lines on the template. The lines are used to place embroidery designs with ease and precision and are essential when you are combining designs or when one design is made up of several smaller designs. It is also important to mark the position of the top of the hoop with a directional arrow on the vertical line; you will need this on both the template and the fabric for each design.

8   *Summer Wine* is an embroidered quilt that combines several designs to make one large design. When you need two or more embroidery designs to make one large embroidery motif or a combination of embroideries, the templates for each design section are printed, roughly cut out, combined and then held together with sticky tape, with positioning holes punched in the center of each separate embroidery design template. Again, mark the position of the top of the hoop for each design on each template and on the fabric.

These pictures illustrate the sequence in which the templates are used for the top and bottom panel of *Summer Wine* quilt.

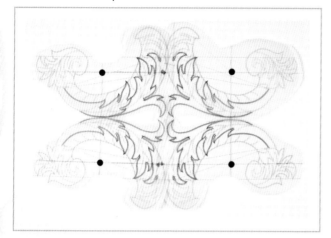

Combining four center scroll designs

Combining two flower designs to make one long spray

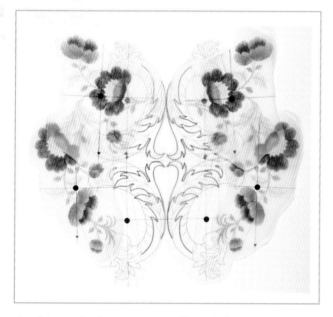

Combining the four center scrolls with the two long flower spays

By doing this you have the center position clearly marked (with vertical and horizontal lines that allow you to keep the fabric straight on the stabilizer in the hoop) for each section of the design. Recheck each section before you commence a new embroidery, and double-check the position of the next design or section carefully – sometimes things move slightly once the fabric is embroidered.

9   Combination templates should also be marked with vertical and horizontal lines that intersect through the center of the combination template design, and these lines should then be referenced to those marked on the fabric you will be embroidering. This ensures that the design is centered and positioned inside the marked cutting edge of the fabric.

SELF-ADHESIVE TEAR-AWAY STABILIZER

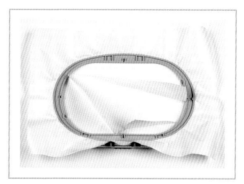

10   Use paper scissors to cut a piece of self-adhesive tear-away stabilizer that is 1½in wider and longer than the hoop it is being used for. Hoop the stabilizer as you would fabric, with the protective coating uppermost in the hoop.

TIP *from the Winemaker*:
Cut a good supply of stabilizer to hoop size and have it on hand, rather than cutting a piece each time you need it. Purchasing a second hoop for your machine is a good idea – that way the next hoop is ready to go once you have completed an embroidery.

11   Use a pin or sharp object to score diagonal lines (that pierce the protective coating only) that intersect through the center of the stabilizer in the hoop, as well as around the inside of the hoop. Next, use a pin to lift each of the four sections of protective coating from the center (these should come off easily with the help of the score lines).

12   Next, call the design up onto the screen. Make sure it is in the center of the screen and the needle is in the center of the design.

13 Place the hoop in the machine, then place the fabric to be embroidered over the sticky stabilizer in the hoop so the intersecting placement lines match those marked on the hoop and the needle sits at the point where the two lines intersect. Also make sure that the mark you made on the fabric for the top of the hoop matches the top of the actual hoop once the fabric is placed on the stabilizer.

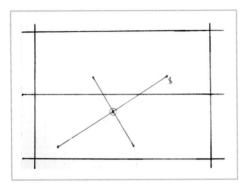

14 The idea of using sticky stabilizer in the hoop is so you can move the fabric on the stabilizer rather than the design on the screen. It also saves re-hooping fabric time and time again, and helps to achieve accurate placement with ease.

15 To double-check that you have the fabric square centered over the stabilizer and hoop, use the following accurate placement technique on your Bernina machine:

(a) Put the hoop (with sticky stabilizer in it) in the machine. Select your chosen embroidery design.

(b) When the chosen embroidery design appears on the screen, the default screen is *Screen No 1* of the two **editing screens**, and the needle defaults to the start of the embroidery design.

(c) Select the hoop size by touching the **hoop** icon (the top-left icon on the screen) on the drop-down hoop screen. Touch **check module** (the hoop will move in the machine), then select **oval 145mm x 255mm** hoop. The screen will again return to *Screen No 1* of the **editing screen**.

(d) Touch the **centering** icon (the third icon on the left side of the screen – a circle with a + in the middle of it) to center the needle in the design. Place the fabric over the sticky stabilizer in the hoop so that the point where the vertical and horizontal lines intersect (this is marked on the fabric) sits exactly under the needle, and the vertical and horizontal lines marked on the fabric match those on the hoop.

(e) Touch the **next screen** icon (a hand symbol pointing to *Screen No 2*) to get to the next screen. This is the **editing screen**.

(f) There are two vertical rows of **editing icons** down the right side of the screen. Touch the **moving** icon (this is the top left icon that has vertical, horizontal and diagonal lines with directional arrows).

(g) When the **moving** icon is active it is highlighted, and the **vertical** (stitch length) and horizontal (stitch width) controls appear on the left of the **moving** icon on the screen. The actual controls on the machine are now activated.

(h) By turning the **vertical** (stitch length) control knob, the needle (and design, but don't worry about this) moves up and down the screen and hoop, vertically centered, thus tracking up and down over the vertical marked line on the fabric over the stabilizer in the hoop.

(i) If the fabric is placed straight in the hoop, the needle should track exactly over the marked vertical line on the fabric. If it doesn't, move the fabric so the vertical line marked on the fabric aligns with the one the needle is tracking.

(j) Touch the **moving** icon to bring the needle (and the design on screen) back to the center of the hoop and fabric.

(k) Repeat steps (f) and (g) for the horizontal line, then touch the **moving** icon to bring the needle and design back to the center of the fabric and hoop.

(l) Touch the **next screen** icon to return to the *Screen No 1* editing screen, then touch **OK** at the bottom right-hand corner of the screen. This takes you to the **embroidery/sew screen** to stitch out the design.

16 Use a complete new piece of sticky stabilizer for each new embroidery. By doing this, the fabric is held firm and stable, thus ensuring perfect embroidery results.

FABRIC AND BATTING

TIP *from the Winemaker*:
The 'glue' on the back of the *Quilt Magic* lightweight fusible batting is a steam and heat-activated bond. To make sure the batting is completely fused to the back of the fabric (and if your iron does not generate enough steam), use a light spray of water; the fabric needs to be totally and evenly secured to the batting as if they are one fabric. If the batting is not secured firmly to the back of the fabric, the fabric will move during embroidery, causing the embroidery design to distort and the fabric to pucker.

17 Use a hot steam iron to fuse the piece of *Quilt Magic* lightweight fusible batting (which is a matching size) to the back of each quilt section.

18   Stabilize each block by using three coats of
heavy-duty spray starch, ironing between coats.

EMBROIDERY

Note: Each embroidered section of the
Summer Wine quilt can stand alone, to be made into
pillows, a wall-hanging, a tablecloth or a runner.
Vary the colors to suit your decor.

19   It is recommended that your machine be
serviced before you start this quilt, and that it is kept
cleaned and oiled during the quilt's embroidery
and construction.

20   Helmar's *Dust-a-way* is great for keeping lint
away from the bobbin and needle tension areas of
your machine.

21   All embroidery uses the Bernina *Gold Latch*
bobbin case, as the tension is (or can be) tightened
when you use a fine thread in the bobbin. We've also
used *Robison-Anton* rayon 40 embroidery threads in
a Jeans 80 needle, darning foot No 26, the basting
stitch downloaded from the Bernina USA website
and sticky stabilizer in the hoop.

22   Use a fine Bobbinfil thread in the bobbin – it is
an essential ingredient for achieving perfect
embroidery, as the finer the bobbin thread the less
bulk there is in any embroidery. A fine bobbin thread
can reduce the embroidery bulk by up to one-third,
ensuring flat, smooth embroidery with little or no
fabric puckering.

23   *Robison-Anton* rayon 40 embroidery threads
ensure a shimmering and perfect embroidery result,
and they offer a range of colors that is second to none
in the market. The subtle change of thread colors in
the flowers and leaves in *Summer Wine* makes the
embroidery glisten as one color seems to run into
another. The way the thread colors are used in the
flower and leaf embroidery also appears to give them
a three-dimensional effect.

24   Embroidered appliqué is used in some of the
embroidery designs:

Step No 1. The Appliqué outline is sewn.

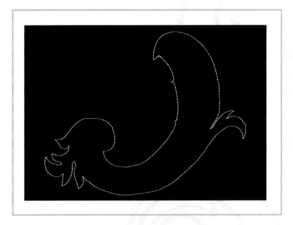

Step No 2. Place the appliqué fabric (backed with fusible
web) over the outline, then stitch the outline again.

Step No 3. Remove the hoop from the machine
(not the fabric from hoop) and use small sharp scissors
to carefully cut around the outside edge of the row
of stitching.

Step No 4. Place the fabric back in the machine.

Step No 5. Machine-embroider around the cut fabric edges of the appliqué fabric.

All embroidery is done in a particular sequence, which is given for each fabric section of the quilt. Be sure to follow the sequence when you are embroidering combination designs.

25   When you position each embroidery design template, note the position that the design sits on the block and whether it is alongside or overlapping the previous embroidered design. It is important to be accurate so that the combination of the embroidered designs appear as one design.

26   Always refer to the picture and the embroidery layout of each quilt section to check embroidery positions, and the direction the motif is facing on the fabric. Be careful not to embroider too close to (no closer than ½in) or over the marked border lines that denote the seam line of each section.

27   After each embroidery design is complete and before you start the next one:

—clip the bobbin thread at intervals from the back of the basting stitch, then pull the needle thread from the top of the fabric to remove the basting stitch

—remove all excess stabilizer from the back of each design

—clip all jump threads and press each embroidery design

—reposition the combination template over the quilt section, matching vertical and horizontal divide lines on the combination template with those marked on the quilt section. Make sure the template design/s sit over the design/s already embroidered on the quilt section; you need this to be right before you can accurately check the position of the next embroidery design.

28   Use water in a spray bottle to spray each quilt section when all the embroidery is complete. This should remove the fabric-marking pen lines. Spray the water generously and evenly over the fabric, then lay the section flat and allow it to dry naturally. Press it and then label each section.

We are now ready to harvest the grapes to make our Summer Wine, so that they can be pressed and allowed to mature grapefully. We wait anxiously for the wine's coming of age …

The color *bouquet and taste of wine*

*Wine, as we know, is judged
by its color, bouquet and taste
(appealing to three of our most commonly used senses —
sight, smell and taste).*

If we liken the wine color to the fabric color, the bouquet to the threads and the taste to the overall effect of a quilt, we can see that all three elements are integral parts, contributing to the overall success of a quilt.

Color is my passion — it is what inspires, attracts and excites me — not to mention any bouquet or taste. They all seem to come together with glorious harmony, but if one element were to be missing, the whole thing would fail.

To guide you in selecting your fabrics and threads (if you'd rather not use the ones we've used), we have combined some luscious combinations to inspire and excite your creative spirit. So go ahead, choose your favorite wine!

Note: All these color combinations can be used with off-white or ivory as a background fabric. The threads listed are Robison-Anton colors and numbers.

PURPLE GRAPE

Heather (No 2271), Tulip (No 2286), Laurie Lilac (No 2425), Dark Purple (No 2381), Plum Wine (No 2490), Brown (No 2251), Tamarak (No 2230), Cypress (No 2545) and Metallic Gold (No 1003)

PLUM WINE

TH Burgundy (No 2608), Warm Wine (No 2496), Dark Maroon (No 2376),
Intense Maroon (No 2587), Earthen Tan (No 2569), Sun Shadow (No 2548), Tamarak (No 2230)
and Euro Metallic Gold

RED GRAPE

Cranberry (No 2270), Coral Red (No 2268), Red Jubilee (No 2421),
Warm Wine (No 2496), Brown (No 2251), Cypress (No 2545),
Desert Cactus (No 2544) and Antique Metallic Gold

ICED WINE

Traditional Grey (No 2540), Ivory (No 2335), Cottage Beige (No 2593), Amber Beige (No 2336), Wicker (No 2489), Palm Leaf (No 2241) and Willow (No 2221)

GOLDEN WINE

Penny (No 2332), 14 KT Gold (No 2586), Ginger (No 2333), Mustard (No 2331), Earthen Tan (No 2569), Foliage Green (No 2542), Desert Cactus (No 2544) and Euro Metallic Gold

ROSÉ

Light Pink (No 2243), Pink (No 2223), Rose Tint (No 2591), Wild Pink (No 2259), Bone (No 2582), Cottage Beige (No 2593), Pistachio (No 2250) and Snow White (No 2297)

STRAWBERRY WINE

nson (No 2416), Strawberry (No 2432), Cherry Punch (No 2417), Cherrystone (No 2504), Amber
Beige (No 2336), Peapod (No 2456), Crescent Moon (No 2546) and Snow White (No 2297)

Taste testing
Summer Wine pillow

est the sweetness of the grapes taken straight from the vine; anticipate making your *Summer Wine* quilt with this indulgent little pillow using one of the designs from the *Summer Wine* quilt design CD.

Making this pillow will ensure we all understand the techniques used in the *Summer Wine* quilt – they will give you experience and the confidence you need before you start on the quilt.

Note: The *Summer Wine* silk and Robison-Anton *Summer Wine* thread collection are available from Quilters' Resource in the US.

Materials

- Bernina *Arista 730E* sewing machine and embroidery module
- Oval embroidery hoop (145mm x 255mm)
- Bernina embroidery software *Version 5* and transfer device
- *Summer Wine* design CD (included free with this book)
- One 12in square of ivory silk dupion for center panel of pillow
- Two 2in x 11¼in strips of antique green silk dupion for narrow borders
- 12in strip across the width of burgundy silk dupion for 4in border strips and pillow backing
- Small piece of black silk dupion for appliqué
- Small piece of double-sided fusible web to back appliqué fabric
- One-yard roll of Jenny's *Quilt Magic* lightweight fusible batting
- 12in x 3in-wide looped ribbon braid (available from Spotlight in Australia and Joanne's in the US)
- One 10in x 16in pillow insert
- Machine feet: embroidery foot/darning foot No 26, BSR (Bernina Stitch Regulator) (these two feet come with the machine), open-toe appliqué foot No 20 and ¼in patchwork foot No 37
- Machine needles: Jeans size 80
- Bernina *Gold Latched* bobbin case (this comes with the machine) for embroidery
- Threads: Robison-Anton rayon 40 embroidery threads in the following colors: Salmon (No 2299), Warm Wine (No 2496), Passion Rose (No 2499), TH Burgundy (No 2608), Dark Maroon (No 2376), Golden Tan (No 2570), Pistachio (No 2250), Olive Drab (No 2317), Black (No 2296) and Metallic Gold (No 1003)
- Bobbinfil, 80 weight, to wind Bernina bobbins
- Bernina metal bobbins
- Cream construction thread for needle and bobbins
- *Hoop Magic*, Jenny's self-adhesive tear-away stabilizer for embroidery backing
- Heavy-duty spray starch
- Water-soluble fabric-marking pen
- Rotary cutter, self-healing cutting mat and quilting ruler
- Small sharp scissors to cut out appliqué
- Glass-headed quilting pins
- Spray bottle for water to remove placement marks
- Good surge of steam iron
- General sewing requirements

PREPARATION

1   Use the self-healing cutting mat, quilting ruler and rotary cutter to cut the following:

from the ivory silk dupion and *Quilt Magic* lightweight fusible batting:

—one, 12in square for the center of the pillow top; cut two squares of the batting

from the antique green silk dupion and *Quilt Magic* lightweight fusible batting:

—two, 2in x 11¼in strips for the narrow side borders of the pillow center

from the burgundy silk dupion and *Quilt Magic* lightweight fusible batting

—two, 4in x 11¼in strips for the wide side borders of the pillow

from the burgundy silk dupion only:

—one, 30in x 11¼in strip for the pillow backing.

2   Use a hot steam iron to press the batting to the back of the matching sized fabric pieces; also fuse the double-sided fusible web to the back of the black silk fabric to be used for the appliqué.

3   Stabilize the ivory silk 12in square with several coats of heavy-duty spray starch, ironing between coats.

4   Use the fabric-marking pen and quilting ruler to mark vertical and horizontal lines that intersect at the center of the ivory silk 12in square. (This is a good way to test your fabric-marking pen, to make sure it can be removed with water once the pillow is complete.)

5   Wind two Bernina bobbins with Bobbinfil.

EMBROIDERY

Use the embroidery foot, the Gold Latched bobbin case, a Jeans 80 needle threaded with Robison-Anton rayon 40 embroidery thread, the Bernina bobbin wound with Bobbinfil and *Hoop Magic* sticky stabilizer in the oval embroidery hoop.

6   Refer to pages 10–14 to download the basting stitch from the Bernina website to place around the embroidery design.

7   Use the Bernina software and transfer device to transfer design **sw19** with the basting stitch around it from the *Summer Wine* design CD (included with this book) to the machine.

8   Embroider design **sw19** centered on the ivory silk 12in square backed with fusible batting, using the black silk for the appliqué fabric.

9   The following are the thread stops and color sequence for **sw19**:

⠀Color 1⠀⠀Black (No 2296)⠀⠀Scroll outline

Place the black fabric backed with double-sided fusible web over the design outline.

⠀Color 2⠀⠀Black (No 2296)⠀⠀Scroll outline

Remove the hoop from the machine (not the fabric from the hoop), then use small sharp scissors to carefully cut out the appliqué fabric close to and parallel to the row of stitching. Place the hoop back in the machine.

	Color	Thread	Area
	Color 3	Metallic Gold (No 1003)	Appliqué stitch
	Color 4	TH Burgundy (No 2608)	Appliqué stitch
	Color 5	Olive Drab (No 2317)	Small leaves
	Color 6	Golden Tan (No 2570)	Stem
	Color 7	Pistachio (No 2250)	Large leaves
	Color 8	Warm Wine (No 2496)	Back petals
	Color 9	TH Burgundy (No 2608)	Shading back petals
	Color 10	Passion Rose (No 2499)	Petals
	Color 11	Salmon (No 2299)	Shading front petals
	Color 12	Metallic Gold (No 1003)	Flower center
	Color 13	Passion Rose (No 2499)	Turn-back petal
	Color 14	Golden Tan (No 2570)	Stem

10   Remove the hoop from the machine, then clip the basting stitches and all the jump threads. Carefully tear the stabilizer from the fabric, removing as much stabilizer as possible from the back of the embroidery. Press the embroidery from the front of the fabric.

11   Use water in the spray bottle to remove the pen marks from your work. Allow it to dry naturally, then press it again from the front.

QUILTING

12 Iron the second 12in square of fusible batting to the back of the 12in embroidered ivory silk square. (I have found this to be beneficial when quilting, as it gives more stability and a better loft to your quilting.)

13 Use the Bernina Stitch Regulator (BSR) to quilt in and around the embroidery on the 12in embroidered ivory silk square using the McTavishing quilting design that has been used in the *Summer Wine* quilt. This is a good way to practise your quilting for the quilt, as well as getting to know your *BSR* (which will soon become your best friend).

14 Cut the quilted 12in embroidered square to 11¼in x 8in, keeping the embroidery centered vertically.

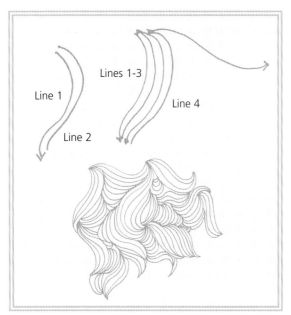

CONSTRUCTION

15 Use construction thread in the needle and bobbin and the ¼in patchwork foot to construct the pillow.

16 Attach the 2in narrow antique green silk borders to each 11¼in side of the embroidered center panel of the pillow, then add the 4in wide burgundy silk borders to the antique green borders. Press the seams to the inside of the antique green border strip.

DECORATIVE STITCHING

17 Use the open-toe appliqué foot No 20, bobbinfil in the bobbin, Dark Maroon (No 2376) in the Jeans 80 needle and paper as stabilizer at the back of the stitching.

18 Select a satin-stitch scallop (width 7, density 0.25 and length 11-12) to sew down each side of the narrow antique green border fabric. The straight edge of the stitch should align with and be parallel to the edge of the antique green fabric with the scallops swinging onto the green fabric. (This decorative

stitching will sew over the seams on the back of the pillow.) The scallops should match as best as possible on each side of the antique green border strip.

19 Continue construction by cutting the 30in x 11¼in burgundy fabric strip in half lengthwise (two, 15in x 11¼in rectangles). On the two 11¼in sides of each burgundy piece of pillow backing fabric, turn under a 1in hem.

20 Overlap the two hemmed burgundy silk backing fabric pieces. The wrong sides of the top pieces should be facing the right side of the underneath fabric, with the hemmed edges facing the outside edge of the pillow and the overlapped fabric pieces forming an 11¼in x 17½in rectangle. Use the glass-headed pins to pin down the overlaps along the raw fabric edges, then stitch them together with a narrow hem along the raw fabric overlap edge only.

21 Place the overlapped pillow backing fabric over the pillow front, right sides together, then pin around the edges and sew around all four sides.

22 Turn the pillow to the right side, making sure the corners are pushed all the way out, and then press both the pillow front and back.

23 On the right side of the pillow, attach the 3in-wide looped ribbon braid to each narrow end.

24 Place the 10in x 16in insert in the pillow.

How did you enjoy your first sips of Summer Wine? You are now a seasoned winemaker and ready to bring out your own private Summer Wine label! Now you can start picking your grapes with confidence, and enjoy the 'grape' anticipation of a wonderful vintage as you start making your personal Summer Wine quilt.

TURN TO THE BACK OF THE BOOK for other exciting ways to use these wonderful designs, with the *Spring Wine* collection of pillows, mirror, table and chairs, as well as a foot warmer, pillow shams and a table quilt, which introduce a new technique called *Embroidery Decoupage*. This is easy, fun and can be used on furniture, home decor and easy bedroom accessories. All these projects are quick and easy and open up a whole new way of using machine embroidery.

The Bernina Stitch Regulator (BSR)

is a revolutionary foot that attaches to a domestic sewing/embroidery machine, world patented and exclusive to Bernina, designed to fit model numbers 440, 630, 640 200 and 730. This amazing attachment allows a freehand machine-quilter to master in minutes what used to require hours of practice – that is, consistent free-motion stitching.

The BSR attachment takes the fear factor out of free-motion machine-quilting, as it automatically regulates the stitch length (all stitches have the same length), adjusting the stitch length in direct ratio to the speed at which the quilter moves the fabric under the needle. This results in free-motion stitching/quilting that has uniform stitch lengths.

Working well with all types and sizes of fabric, the BSR comes with variable speed, adjustable stitch length and width (on machine models with zigzag BSR) as well as the option of 'cruise control' – there is no need to use a foot control; instead, the start/stop button on the machine gives the quilting artist the control and freedom to concentrate on exploring creativity.

Using cutting-edge technology with the fine tradition of Bernina quality, the BSR is a foot that attaches to the machine, is light, compact and user friendly, as well as easy to learn and operate. The fabric is moved under the needle rather than the machine over the fabric, which maximizes space at hand and eliminates the need to house a free-standing frame (although it works well with the Aurora range of machines and frames).

The Bernina Stitch Regulator is a must
for any quilter who wants to master free-motion stitching
and quilting, so why wait when the BSR is knocking
at your sewing studio door – all you have to do is open the door
to total BSR free-motion freedom!

Summer *Wine*

Make your life an endless summer by creating your own Summer Wine quilt. With it will come the joy and harmony a winemaker feels when he has created his own vintage Summer Wine, and the knowledge that you have created a timeless masterpiece.

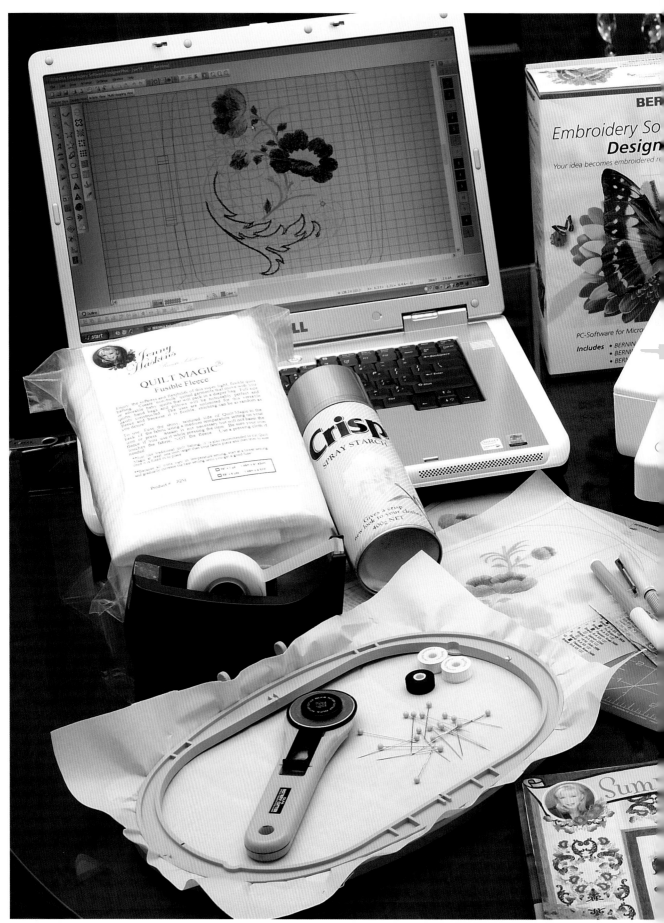

Summer *Wine*

From little things, big things grow

Materials

- Bernina *Arista 730E* sewing machine and embroidery module
- Oval embroidery hoop (145mm x 255mm)
- Bernina embroidery software *Version 5* and transfer device
- *Summer Wine* design CD (included free with this book)
- FABRIC:
  6½yd x 45in ivory silk dupion for embroidery
  3yd x 45in burgundy silk dupion for wide borders and binding
  2½yd x 45in antique green silk dupion for narrow borders
  2yd x 45in black silk for appliqué
  6yd x 45in cream backing fabric
- 5yd x 60in *Quilt Magic* (Jenny's lightweight fusible batting)
- 3yd x 36in double-sided fusible web
- Machine feet: embroidery foot/darning foot No 26, *BSR* (Bernina Stitch Regulator) – these two feet come with the machine – and ¼ patchwork foot with guide No 37
- Machine needles: Jeans size 80
- Bernina *Gold Latched* bobbin case (this comes with the machine) for embroidery
- THREADS:
  Robison-Anton rayon 40 embroidery threads in the following colors: Salmon (No 2299), Warm Wine (No 2496), Passion Rose (No 2499), TH Burgundy (No 2608), Golden Tan (No 2570), Pistachio (No 2250), Olive Drab (No 2317), Black (No 2296) and Metallic Gold (No 1003)
- Bobbinfil, 80 weight, to wind Bernina bobbins
- 10 Bernina metal bobbins
- Cream and burgundy construction thread for needle and bobbins
- Hoop Magic self-adhesive tear-away stabilizer for embroidery backing
- 50 sheets of vellum tracing paper to print placement templates
- Sticky tape to hold templates together
- Awl hole punch to piece templates
- Two cans of heavy-duty spray starch to stabilize fabric to be embroidered
- Three water-soluble fabric-marking pens
- Rotary cutter, self-healing cutting mat and quilting ruler
- Lead pencil to mark templates
- Paper scissors to cut out templates
- Small sharp scissors to cut out appliqué
- Kai cutting shears
- Glass-headed quilting pins
- Spray bottle for water to remove placement marks
- Good surge of steam iron
- Hand-sewing needle
- Helmar's *Dust-a-way* to clean lint from machine
- General sewing requirements

PREPARATION

Cutting

1   Use the rotary cutter, self-healing cutting mat and quilting ruler to cut from the:

ivory silk dupion and *Quilt Magic* fusible batting:

> **Note:** The cutting measurements for the ivory silk dupion are for the fabric to be embroidered on. The fabric will be cut to piecing size once all the embroidery is complete.

—four, 20in squares for each corner of the quilt

—four, 20in x 26in rectangles for the sides of the quilt

—two, 20in x 33in rectangles for the top and bottom of the quilt

—two, 24in x 27in rectangles for the center medallion

antique green silk dupion and *Quilt Magic* fusible batting:

—two, 1½in x 27in strips for the narrow outer top and bottom borders of the center medallion

—two, 1½in x 44½in strips for the narrow side borders of the center medallion

—two, 1½in x 59in strips for the narrow top and bottom quilt borders

—two, 1½in x 59in strips for the narrow side quilt borders

burgundy silk dupion and *Quilt Magic* fusible batting:

—two, 2½in x 23in strips for the wide top and bottom inner borders of the center medallion

—two, 2½in x 42½in strips for the wide side inner borders of the center medallion

—two, 6in x 62in strips for the top and bottom quilt borders

—two, 6in x 89in strips for the side quilt borders

burgundy silk dupion only:

—2½in strips on the straight across the width or length of the fabric, joined on the bias to measure 9½yd, for the quilt binding.

2   Use a hot steam iron to fuse the batting to the back of all the matching sized fabric pieces, then label them and put all the border and binding pieces to one side. Also iron the double-sided fusible web to the back of the black silk fabric that will be used for the appliqué fabric in the embroidery designs.

3   Use several coats of the heavy-duty spray starch to stabilize all the ivory silk fabric pieces backed with fusible batting. Iron between each coat.

4   Use the water-soluble fabric-marking pen and quilting ruler to mark all the ivory fabric pieces backed with fusible batting with vertical, horizontal and diagonal lines that intersect at the center.

5   Refer to the *Cut to Piecing* Size layout diagram (on page 52), then use the quilting ruler and fabric-marking pen to mark the cutting edge on each piece of ivory silk dupion backed with fusible batting. This will keep your embroidery well clear of the cutting edge of the fabric. Remember that there is a ¼in seam allowance on all four sides of each fabric piece.

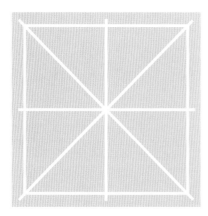

TIP *from the Winemaker:*
You can wind a bobbin on the Bernina
while it is embroidering, so it is a good idea to fill
your bobbins as they become empty
and while the machine is embroidering.

6   Use the Bernina Embroidery software *Version 5* and transfer device to transfer the embroidery designs from the *Summer Wine* design CD to the sewing machine on a need-to-use basis, as well as printing design placement templates on the vellum tracing paper.

7   Use the awl to punch placement holes in each vellum design template and the lead pencil to mark the direction of the top of the hoop on each one.

8   Wind the 10 Bernina bobbins with the Bobbinfil you will be using for the embroidery.

The sections of the quilt to be embroidered:

- corner squares
- top and bottom borders
- side borders
- center medallion

The instructions are given for each section in the order noted above. Refer to the techniques and tips on pages 10–14 at all times, as well as pages 96–102 for the individual designs where the thread stops and colors used are listed.

Take your time, starting with the corner squares. When you have mastered these you are well on your way. You have done all the groundwork, the vines are loaded, so go harvest your grapes, remembering that *from little things, big things grow.*

Enjoy the wine-making process;
picking grapes may take some time,
but when the Summer Wine is being sipped it is very sweet.
Start picking and blending your grapes now!

Top of quilt

CORNER SQUARES

CORNER SQUARES TO BE JOINED TO THE TOP AND BOTTOM OF THE QUILT SIDE SECTIONS (to make the top and bottom quilt panels)

Quilt section pieces: Nos 7, 9, 10 and 12

> **Note:** To ensure success, refer at all times to the picture of the quilt (page 31), the *Cut to Piecing* layout diagram (page 52), the *Cellar Master's Winning Formula* (preparation, tips and techniques: pages 10 to 14) and the *Wine List* (*Summer Wine* designs with thread stops and color sequence: pages 96 to 102).

Use the four 20in squares of ivory silk backed with batting in the four corners of the *Summer Wine* quilt. The quilt piecing sequence for these four squares is No 7, No 9, No 10 and then No 12.

1   Use the fabric-making pen and quilting ruler to mark a 14in square centered in the 20in square. This square will mark the outside edge of the combination template; no part of any embroidery design should extend past this square.

2   Use the Bernina embroidery software, the *Summer Wine* design CD and the transfer device to transfer the following designs to the machine:

—**sw01** embroidery sequence No 1; centered so the 'points' of the design sit over the vertical and horizontal divide lines in the 20in square

—**sw02** embroidery sequence Nos 2, 3, 4 and 5; centered so each appliqué scroll touches the vertical and horizontal divide lines

—**sw03** embroidery sequence Nos 6, 7, 8 and 9; centered over the four **sw02** designs

—**sw04** embroidery sequence Nos 10, 11, 12 and 13; centered above and overlapping the intersection of the appliqué scrolls.

3   Use your *Summer Wine* design CD, embroidery software, PC, printer and vellum tracing paper to print four templates for each design *except* **sw01** (as this is the first design and centered in the square, there is no need to print a template for it).

4   Use the block embroidery design layout to combine the templates, and then use sticky tape to hold them together.

5   The black text on the block embroidery design layout represents the file name of the designs, and the red numbers represent the embroidery sequence.

6   Embroider all four 20in squares following the embroidery sequence given in step 2.

7   When all the embroidery is complete, clip all jump threads from the front and back, remove all excess stabilizer from the back, then press the blocks, labeling the top of each one to avoid confusion.

Top of quilt

13 sw07

15 sw07

sw05 sw05

sw05 sw05

12 sw06

10 sw06

6

7

4

2

9 sw06

11 sw06

1

3

sw05 sw05

sw05 sw05

16 sw07

14 sw07

8

5

CENTER PANEL FOR THE TOP AND BOTTOM OF THE QUILT

Quilt section pieces: Nos 8 and 11

> **Note:** To ensure success, refer at all times
> to the picture of the quilt (page 31),
> the *Cut to Piecing* layout diagram (page 52),
> the *Cellar Master's Winning Formula*
> (preparation, tips and techniques: pages 10 to 14)
> and the *Wine List* (*Summer Wine* designs with
> thread stops and color sequence: pages 96 to 102).

Use the two 20in x 33in rectangles of ivory silk
backed with batting for the center panel of the top and
bottom sections of the *Summer Wine* quilt. Follow the
piecing sequence of No 8 and then No 11.

1   Use the fabric-making pen and quilting ruler to
mark a 14½in x 24¾in rectangle centered in the 20in
x 33in rectangle. This rectangle will mark the outside
edge of the combination template; no part of any
embroidery design should extend past this rectangle.

2   Also use the fabric-marking pen and quilting
ruler to divide each half of the silk rectangle vertically
in half again. The rectangle is now divided vertically
into quarters.

3   Use the Bernina embroidery software, the
Summer Wine design CD and the transfer device to
transfer the following designs to the machine:

—**sw05** embroidery sequence Nos 1 to 8.
These appliqué scrolls are embroidered in groups of
two, on each side of the horizontal divide line on the
20in x 33in silk rectangle, so the points touch to form
four elongated 'heart' shapes

—**sw06** embroidery sequence Nos 9 to 12; the upper
section of the four flower swags, one on each side
of the scrolls so the blunt top end of the stem touches
the appliqué scroll (**sw05**)

—**sw07** embroidery sequence Nos 13 to 17; the bottom overlapping section of the flower swag, with the bottom blunt end of the stem touching the appliqué scroll (**sw05**).

> **Note:** With this type of combination design, the individual designs are embroidered opposite each other rather than in a clockwise or anti-clockwise direction. This makes any placement errors easier to correct.

4   Use your *Summer Wine* design CD, embroidery software, PC, printer and vellum tracing paper to print four templates for **sw05** (remember to mirror the designs horizontally and vertically as you need them), two templates for **sw06** (mirrored horizontally or vertically as needed) and two templates for **sw07** (again mirrored horizontally and vertically as needed).

5   Use half of the center top and bottom embroidery design layout to combine the templates (this is half of the design layout, from the center vertical to one end), then use sticky tape to hold the templates together. Fold the combination template in half vertically and horizontally, then use the lead pencil and quilting ruler to mark the fold lines. These lines should match the ones marked on the fabric *at all times* when you are marking the placement positions for each individual embroidery design.

6   When you are replacing the template over the fabric once each design has been embroidered, the template design should sit over the embroidered one. If you find that the vertical and horizontal marked lines on the combination template do not match those marked on the fabric, correct it as you mark placement positions for the next design. This will keep the combination embroidery design square and straight.

7   The way the embroidery designs have been combined and subsequently stitched is very forgiving, as the designs overlap each other, but the whole combination design should be kept straight, both vertically and horizontally, to ensure a pleasing end result.

8   This combination template is used for each side of the silk rectangle with the appliqué designs touching at the three vertical divide lines and almost touching on the horizontal divide line. It will need to be flipped over when you mark the embroidery positions for the opposite end of the design sequence.

9   The black text on the center top and bottom embroidery design layout represents the file name of the designs, and the red numbers represent the embroidery sequence.

10   Embroider the two 20in x 33in rectangles following the embroidery sequence given in step 3. Check the position and direction (mirrored horizontally or vertically) of all the embroidery designs to ensure the design on the screen of the sewing machine matches that of the template. *Rule of thumb:* Check embroidery position and direction twice and embroider once!

11   When all the embroidery is complete, clip all jump threads from the front and back, remove all excess stabilizer from the back, then press the top and bottom quilt panels, labeling the top of each one to avoid confusion.

Halfway through *the harvest*

8
sw08

9
sw08

sw09
10

sw05
6

sw05
7

13
sw08

14
sw08

sw10
1

sw10
2

4
sw02

5
sw02

sw12
11

sw12
12

sw11
3

SIDE SECTIONS (two sections joined for each side) OF THE QUILT

Quilt section pieces: Nos 3, 4, 5 and 6

Note: To ensure success, refer at all times to the picture of the quilt (page 31), the *Cut to Piecing* layout diagram (page 52), the *Cellar Master's Winning Formula* (preparation, tips and techniques: pages 10 to 14) and the *Wine List* (*Summer Wine* designs with thread stops and color sequence: pages 96 to 102).

Use the four 20in x 26in rectangles of ivory silk backed with batting for the two side panels (two sections are joined together for each side panel) of the *Summer Wine* quilt. Follow the piecing sequence of No 3, No 4, No 5 and then No 6.

1   Use the fabric-making pen and quilting ruler to mark a 14in x 20in rectangle centered in each of the four 20in x 26in rectangles. This rectangle will mark the outside edge of the combination template; no part of any embroidery design should extend past this rectangle.

2   Use the Bernina embroidery software, the *Summer Wine* design CD and the transfer device to transfer the following designs to the machine:

—**sw11** embroidery sequence No 3. These large lattice and appliqué scrolls sit at the bottom (and/or top) of the center seam of the combination design and over the stems of **sw10**

—**sw02** embroidery sequence Nos 4 and 5; appliqué scrolls on each side of the large scrolls and lattice (**sw11**)

—**sw10** embroidery sequence Nos 1 and 2. The large leaves and stem will sit under the flower designs (**sw08** and **sw12**), and at the top of and under the point of design **sw11**

—**sw05** embroidery sequence Nos 6 and 7; appliqué scrolls on each side of the rectangle above the large leaves of **sw10**

44

—**sw08** embroidery sequence Nos 8 and 9; flower sprays embroidered on each side of the rectangle overlapping the large scroll (**sw05**)

—**sw09** embroidery sequence No 10; centered over the horizontal divide line at the top (and/or bottom) of each side section of the quilt and over the stems of **sw08**

—**sw12** embroidery sequence Nos 11 and 12; on each side of the large leaves sitting over the leaves (**sw10**), above the scrolls and lattice (**sw11**), and over the side scrolls (**sw02**)

—**sw08** embroidery sequence Nos 13 and 14; so the flowers sit over the stems of **sw10** and the top flowers touch on the center vertical line.

> **Note:** With this type of combination design, the individual designs are embroidered opposite each other rather than in a clockwise or anti-clockwise direction. This makes any placement errors easier to correct.

3   Use your *Summer Wine* design CD, embroidery software, PC, printer and vellum tracing paper to print four templates for **sw08** (remember to mirror the designs horizontally and/or vertically as you need them), two templates for **sw10**, **sw02**, **sw05** and **sw12** (remember to mirror the second design horizontally and/or vertically as needed), and one template each for **sw09** and **sw11**.

4   Combine the templates using the side panels embroidery design layout as a guide, then use sticky tape to hold them together. Fold the combination template in half vertically and horizontally, then use the lead pencil and quilting ruler to mark the fold lines. These lines should match the ones marked on the fabric *at all times* when you are marking the placement positions for each individual embroidery design.

5   When you are replacing the template over the fabric once each design has been embroidered, the template design should sit over the embroidered one. If you find that the vertical and horizontal marked lines on the combination template do not match those marked on the fabric, correct it as you mark placement positions for the next design. This will keep the combination embroidery design square and straight.

6   The way the embroidery designs have been combined and subsequently stitched is very forgiving, as the designs overlap each other, but the whole combination design should be kept straight, both vertically and horizontally, to ensure a pleasing end result.

7   The black text on the side panels embroidery design layout represents the file name of the designs, and the red numbers represent the embroidery sequence.

8   Embroider the four 20in x 26in rectangles following the embroidery sequence given in step 3. Check the position and direction (mirrored horizontally or vertically) of all the embroidery designs to ensure the design on the screen of the sewing machine matches that of the template.

Rule of thumb: Check embroidery position and direction twice and embroider once!

9   When all the embroidery is complete, clip all jump threads from the front and back, remove all excess stabilizer from the back, then press the four side sections (that will be joined later, into two sections with a block on each end to make the quilt side panels), labeling the top and/or bottom of each one to avoid confusion.

The last harvest
of summer

sw15
7

8
sw14

9
sw14

11
sw02

12
sw02

sw11
10

1
sw13

2
sw13

14
sw08

15
sw08

13
sw16

5
sw02

3
sw17

6
sw02

4
sw17

17
sw18

16
sw01

18
sw18

seam line

CENTER MEDALLION

CENTER MEDALLION (two sections) OF THE QUILT
Quilt section pieces: Nos 1 and 2

> **Note:** To ensure success, refer at all times to the picture of the quilt (page 31), the *Cut to Piecing* layout diagram (page 52), the *Cellar Master's Winning Formula* (preparation, tips and techniques: pages 10 to 14) and the *Wine List* (*Summer Wine* designs with thread stops and color sequence: pages 96 to 102).

Use the two 24in x 27in rectangles of ivory silk backed with batting for the center medallion (the two sections are joined together to form the center medallion) of the *Summer Wine* quilt. Follow the piecing sequence of No 1 and then No 2.

1 Use the fabric-making pen and quilting ruler to mark a 17½in x 20½in rectangle centered in each of the two 24in x 27in rectangles. This rectangle will mark the outside edge of the combination template; no part of any embroidery design should extend past this rectangle.

> **Note:** The center medallion is embroidered in two identical sections and then joined together across the center horizontal seam line marked on the design layout. The center of the seam (and medallion) is embroidered over with appliqué design **sw01** and the position where the embroideries meet on each side of the seam line is covered with appliqué design **sw18**.

2 Use the Bernina embroidery software, the *Summer Wine* design CD and the transfer device to transfer the following designs to the machine:

—**sw17** embroidery sequence Nos 3 and 4; the flower spray is embroidered slightly over the appliqué scroll (**sw13**) on the opposite side of the divide line on each side of the rectangle

—**sw02** embroidery sequence Nos 5 and 6; appliqué scrolls on each side of the rectangle sitting over the scroll (**sw13**) and flower spray (**sw17**)

—**sw13** embroidery sequence Nos 1 and 2; the appliqué scroll and flower are embroidered on each side of the rectangle and on each side of the divide line

—**sw15** embroidery sequence No 7; flowers centered at the top (and/or bottom) of the rectangle

48

—**sw14** embroidery sequence Nos 8 and 9; large leaves and stem sprays embroidered lightly down from and on each side of the flowers (**sw15**)

—**sw16** embroidery sequence No 13; arched stems and leaves centered over the divide line at the bottom (and/or top) of each section of the center medallion, with the stems starting at the marked seam line

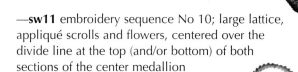

—**sw11** embroidery sequence No 10; large lattice, appliqué scrolls and flowers, centered over the divide line at the top (and/or bottom) of both sections of the center medallion

—**sw08** embroidery sequence Nos 14 and 15; arched flower and buds spray, one on each side of the divide line starting from and sitting above the arched leaves (**sw16**)

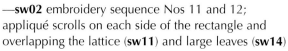

—**sw02** embroidery sequence Nos 11 and 12; appliqué scrolls on each side of the rectangle and overlapping the lattice (**sw11**) and large leaves (**sw14**)

Once the two sections of the center medallion have been joined and the ¼in seam has been ironed open:

—**sw01** embroidery sequence No 16; multiple appliqué design, centered vertically and horizontally over the seam line joining the two embroidered sections of the center medallion

—**sw18** embroidery sequence Nos 17 and 18; single appliqué design centered horizontally on the seam line over the area where the embroidery touches on each side of the seam, pointing to the outside edge of the center medallion.

> **Note:** With this type of combination design, the individual designs are embroidered opposite each other rather than in a clockwise or anti-clockwise direction. This makes any placement errors easier to correct.

3   Use your *Summer Wine* design CD, embroidery software, PC, printer and vellum tracing paper to print two templates for each design (remember to mirror the designs horizontally and/or vertically as you need them), and one template only for **sw11**, **sw15**, **sw16** and **sw01**, then combine the templates using the center medallion embroidery design layout as a guide. Hold the templates together with sticky tape. Fold the combination template in half vertically and horizontally, then use the lead pencil and quilting ruler to mark the fold lines. These lines should match the ones marked on the fabric *at all times* when you are marking the placement positions for each individual embroidery design.

4   When you are replacing the template over the fabric once each design has been embroidered, the template design should sit over the embroidered one. If you find that the vertical and horizontal marked lines on the combination template do not match those marked on the fabric, correct it as you mark placement positions for the next design. This will keep the combination embroidery design square and straight.

5   The way the embroidery designs have been combined and subsequently stitched is very forgiving, as the designs overlap each other, but the whole combination design should be kept straight, both vertically and horizontally, to ensure a pleasing end result.

6   The black text on the center medallion embroidery design layout represents the file name of the designs, and the red numbers represent the embroidery sequence.

7   Embroider the two 24in x 27in rectangles following the embroidery sequence given in step 2. Check the position and direction (mirrored horizontally or vertically) of all the embroidery designs to ensure the design on the screen of the sewing machine matches that of the template. *Rule of thumb:* Check embroidery position and direction twice and embroider once!

8   When both sections of the centre medallion have been embroidered, cut the center seam line to a ¼in allowance from the embroidery, so that when the two sections are seamed the embroideries touch. Don't worry if they are not exactly in line as these areas will be covered with appliqué embroidery designs. Press the seam open.

9   Embroider **sw01** centered in the medallion over the seam line (covering the spot where the stems meet from each section) and **sw18** (covering the spot where the flower buds meet from each section).

10   When all the embroidery is complete, clip all jump threads from the front and back, remove all excess stabilizer from the back, then press the center medallion of the quilt, labeling the top and/or bottom to avoid confusion.

You are now ready
to blend the grapes

Note: All measurements are 'cut to fabric piecing size' and include a ¼in seam.

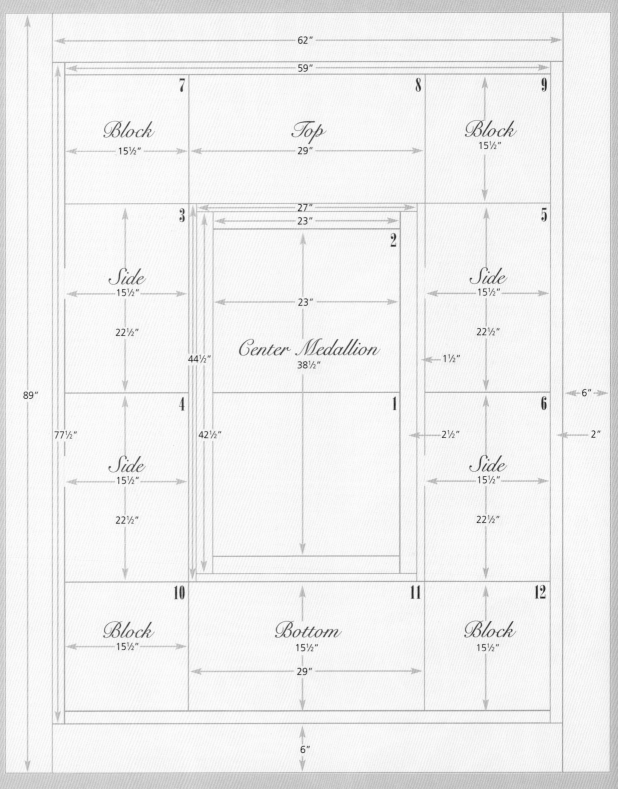

Measurements in inches (eg 15½") are cut to piecing size.
Names represent the quilt section names.
Numbers in red represent piecing sequence.

Blending the grapes
Putting it together

EMBROIDERED QUILT SECTIONS

> **Note:** Refer to the *Summer Wine* quilt picture on page 31 and the *Cut to Piecing Size* layout diagram at all times as you cut quilt sections to piecing size.

> **TIP** *from the Winemaker.*
> Measurements of any quilt may vary depending on how accurately each quilt section has been cut and then pieced.
> Please check all your actual quilt measurements against those given in the instructions, and remember, measure twice as you can only cut once!

CUTTING

1   As embroidery tends to shrink and distort fabric, it is advisable to remeasure and mark all cutting lines on each quilt section.

2   To ensure the embroidery is centered in each section of the quilt, use the quilting ruler to measure out half the cutting width (on each side of the center vertical divide line) and half the cutting length (on each side of the center horizontal line) on all the quilt sections **except** the four side panels. Mark this measurement with a point at intervals along the edges of each embroidered quilt section, then use the quilting ruler and fabric-marking pen to join these points together. This straight line represents the cutting edges of the quilt section.

3   On the four side panels, measure half the cutting width on each side of the center vertical line as you did in step 2. For the length of each panel, measure out $^1/_2$in from the embroidery on the center seam edge and mark a line that is parallel to and $^1/_2$in away from the edge of the embroidered leaves, then measure from this line the length of the embroidery that corresponds to the cut length of each panel ($22^1/_2$in). The embroidery in the side panels is not exactly centered, but when the panels are joined the embroidery is centered in the side sections of the quilt.

4   Once the cutting edges are marked on all the quilt sections, double-check that the marked measurements match those on the *Cut to Piecing Size* layout diagram.

5   Use the wonderfully light and sharp Kai cutting shears to cut cleanly and accurately along the marked cutting lines on each quilt section.

6   Cut the quilt sections to *piecing size* measurements, keeping the labels for each quilt section and the top of the quilt marked:

- blocks (x4): $15^1/_2$in square
- top and bottom panels (x2): $15^1/_2$in x 29in
- side panels (x4): $15^1/_2$in x $22^1/_2$in
- pieced center medallion (x1): 23in x $38^1/_2$in

7   The center medallion and quilt border fabric cutting measurements are given in the preparation section, following the materials list on page 30. Make sure the measurements for these border strips match yours and/or the ones on the *Cut to Piecing Size* layout diagram.

PIECING THE QUILT SECTIONS INTO PANELS

8   Use construction thread in the needle and bobbin and the $^1/_4$in patchwork foot to piece the quilt. Press each seam open after it has been sewn.

9   Join side section three (3) to side section four (4) across the marked seam line, referring to the *Summer Wine* quilt layout diagram and matching your embroidery to that shown on the diagram. Repeat for sections five (5) and six (6).

10   Join block seven (7) to the edge of section three (3) and block ten (10) to the edge of section four (4) for the left side panel of the quilt, making sure the top of each block is facing the top of the quilt. Then join block nine (9) to the edge of section five (5) and block twelve (12) to the edge of section six (6) for the right side panel of the quilt, again making sure the top of each block is facing the top of the quilt.

> **Note:** All border fabric strips are backed with *Quilt Magic* lightweight fusible batting.

11   Join the borders to the center medallion:

—the two, 2½in x 23in wide inner border burgundy strips to the top and bottom of the center medallion

—the two, 2½in x 42½in wide inner border burgundy strips to the sides of the center medallion

—the two, 1½in x 27in narrow outer border green strips to the top and bottom of the center medallion wide borders

—the two, 1½in x 44½in narrow outer border green strips to the sides of the center medallion wide borders.

12   Join the quilt panels to the borders of the center medallion:

—the two, 15½in x 29in embroidered panels to the top and bottom of the quilt

—the two, 15½in x 74½in pieced side panels to each side of the quilt.

13   Join the borders to the quilt:

—the two, 2in x 59in narrow inner border green strips to the top and bottom of the quilt

—the two, 2in x 59in narrow inner border green strips to the sides of the quilt

—the two, 6in x 62in wide outer border burgundy strips to the top and bottom of the quilt

—the two, 6in x 89in wide outer border burgundy strips to the sides of the quilt.

*The quilt construction is now complete;
the grapes have been blended
and placed in the wine kegs, awaiting
the wine's coming of age.*

QUILTING

14   Cut the 6yd x 45in cream backing fabric into two 3yd lengths, then join them down the center to make a 3yd x 90in rectangle to back the quilt.

15   *Summer Wine* was custom-quilted by Jenny and Kim Bradley (mostly Kim as Jenny ran out of time) using the McTavishing quilting design in and around all the embroidery on the quilt sections and a long-arm sewing machine. The borders were quilted using a long-arm computerized machine with original quilting designs created by Kim. All the seams were stitched-in-the-ditch.

16   Choose to quilt your quilt in a way that best suits your skills, time and pocket, remembering that Bernina now has its magic *BSR* (Bernina Stitch Regulator) foot which has a built-in stitch length regulator that makes it easy to achieve perfect stitch length freehand quilting on a domestic machine.

BINDING

17   Join the 2½in wide burgundy strips cut on the straight across the width or length of the fabric together on the bias to measure 9½yd for the quilt binding. Cut one end at a 45-degree angle, then fold it in half lengthwise (wrong sides together) and press it, making sure the raw fabric edges are aligned and parallel to create a French fold for the binding.

18   Open out the end you have cut at 45 degrees, then turn under a ¼in hem, press the hem to the wrong side of the fabric and re-press the fold in the binding. This will be the end at which you start attaching the binding to the quilt.

19   Make sure the quilt is trimmed and squared after the quilting is complete.

20   For binding this quilt, we have used a ½in seam allowance. Measure ½in in from each side of each corner of the quilt and place a pin in the quilt on the vertical to mark the spot.

21   Find the centre of one side of the right side of the quilt. Put the right side of the binding over the quilt (start with the hemmed edge of the binding) with the raw fabric edges of the binding and the quilt aligned and parallel. Pin the first two inches of the binding to the quilt. Next, with a ¹/₂in seam allowance, construction thread and foot, start attaching the binding to the quilt beyond the pins (this section will be attached to the quilt once the binding is joined at the end).

22   Sew the binding to the quilt until you reach the ¹/₂in pin mark from the first corner, then sew off the fabric at a 45-degree angle to the corner and remove the pin. Remove the quilt from the machine and fold the binding upwards and away from the quilt (the binding will fold back against the row of stitching that is at 45 degrees; see diagram below).

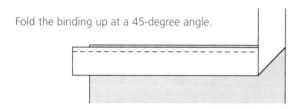

Fold the binding up at a 45-degree angle.

23   Vertically pin-fold the binding (the head of the pin should be to the outside edge of the quilt and aligned with the cut edge of the quilt and binding), then bring the binding in line with the next side edge of the quilt (see diagram below).

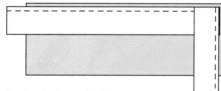

Bring the binding back alongside the next edge, creating a fold at the corner.

24   Bring the quilt back to the machine and start sewing at the top edge, then remove the pins. Continue around the quilt. When the binding reaches 2in from the starting point (of the binding, not the stitching), overlap the end of the binding over the beginning, making sure that it covers (on both sides of the binding and by 1in) the 45-degree angle edge that has been turned under. Cut the end of the binding at the same angle as you did the beginning.

25   Remove the pins from the beginning of the binding and open it out flat. Place the opened-out end over the inside of the beginning of the binding (the right side of the end of the binding is to the wrong side of the beginning of the binding), so the raw fabric edges and the fold lines are aligned. Refold the binding, making sure it is flat. The length of the binding that needs to be sewn to the quilt now measures 4in (or the same as that of the quilt that is left to bind). Pin, making sure the raw fabric edges of the end of the binding are concealed under the hemmed edge of the beginning of the binding.

26   Use a hand-sewing needle to slip-stitch the hemmed edge of the binding overlap.

27   Press and then pin the binding to the back of the quilt. The corners of the binding will automatically form a mitered corner from both the back and front of the quilt. Use a hand-sewing needle to slip-stitch the binding to the back of the quilt, sewing the back mitered corners in place as you go.

28   Sign and date your quilt.

Congratulations, you are now ready to sit in your sunlit summer garden, with the scent of the flowers coming to you on the gentle breeze that floats the butterflies in its currents. It is time to taste the sweetness of your personally blended Summer Wine that has now come of age.

We know you will enjoy sharing your
Summer Wine with your friends and family,
and soaking up the love and adoration that comes
with a successful vintage year.
Summer Wine – a quilt for all seasons!

Introducing *Embroidered Decoupage*

The single most challenging and threatening element of machine embroidery, especially machine-embroidered quilts, is (in my experience) the precise placement of combination embroidery designs on an item. However, once you have mastered precision embroidery placement using the easy methods described in detail on pages 10–14 (using templates, your machine and software functions as well as confidence and experience) it is a breeze.

I do, however, realize that there will always be some who are intimidated by the process, and so *Embroidered Decoupage* is just the thing for those aspiring artists.

Using the following technique, it is possible to include machine embroidery on almost anything, and the really good thing is that the technique is so easy and achievable! The instructions below are for the *Spring Wine* color story used in the *Spring Wine Pillow Duo*, as well as the other projects that follow.

Materials

- Bernina *Arista 730E* sewing machine and embroidery module
- Oval embroidery hoop (145mm x 255mm)
- Bernina embroidery software *Version 5* and transfer device
- *Summer Wine* design CD (included free with this book)
- 14in x 9in piece of sheer light-colored fabric (such as cotton tulle or nylon organza)
- Small piece of lime green gingham fabric for appliqué
- Small piece of double-sided fusible web to back appliqué fabric and embroidery design
- Machine feet: embroidery foot/darning foot No 26
- Machine needles: Jeans size 80
- Bernina *Gold Latched* bobbin case (this comes with the machine) for embroidery
- Threads: Robison-Anton rayon 40 embroidery threads in the following colors:
  Light Pink (No 2243), Pink (No 2223), Rose Tint (No 2591), Wild Pink (No 2259), Bone (No 2582), Cottage Beige (No 2593), Pistachio (No 2250) and Snow White (No 2297)
- Bobbinfil, 80 weight, to wind Bernina bobbins
- Bernina metal bobbins
- *Dissolve Magic*, Jenny's woven soluble stabilizer (two layers used for each hooping)
- Small sharp scissors
- Craft glue (optional)
- Soldering/craft iron (optional)
- Good surge of steam iron
- General sewing requirements

PREPARATION

1   Use the Bernina software, the transfer device and the *Summer Wine* design CD to download design **sw19**.

EMBROIDERY

All embroidery uses the embroidery foot, a size 80 Jeans needle, a metal bobbin wound with bobbinfil, the gold latched bobbin case, the embroidery hoop and Robison-Anton rayon 40 embroidery threads.

2   Place the 14in x 9in piece of sheer fabric in the embroidery hoop with a double layer of the *Dissolve Magic* soluble stabilizer.

3   Embroider design **sw19** on the sheer fabric. The following are the thread stops and color sequence for the design:

🧵   Color 1   Snow White (No 2297)   Scroll outline
Place the lime green gingham fabric backed with double-sided fusible web over the design outline.

🧵   Color 2   Snow White (No 2297)   Scroll outline
Remove the hoop from the machine (not the fabric from the hoop), then use small sharp scissors to carefully cut out the appliqué fabric close to and parallel to the row of stitching. Place the hoop back in the machine.

🧵	Color 3	Pistachio (No 2250)	Appliqué stitch
🧵	Color 4	Snow White (No 2297)	Appliqué stitch
🧵	Color 5	Cottage Beige (No 2593)	Small leaves
🧵	Color 6	Bone (No 2582)	Stem
🧵	Color 7	Pistachio (No 2250)	Large leaves
🧵	Color 8	Wild Pink (No 2259)	Flower petals
🧵	Color 9	Rose Tint (No 2591)	Shading petals
🧵	Color 10	Pink (No 2223)	Front petals
🧵	Color 11	Light Pink (No 2243)	Shading front petals
🧵	Color 12	Snow White (No 2297)	Flower center
🧵	Color 13	Pink (No 2223)	Turn-back petal
🧵	Color 14	Bone (No 2582)	Leaf veins

4   Remove the fabric and the stabilizer from the hoop, then use small sharp scissors to roughly cut away the excess stabilizer from around the embroidery design.

5   Wash the stabilizer from the embroidery by soaking the embroidery design on the sheer fabric in warm water, swishing it regularly. If you are doing a lot of designs, soak them in the laundry tub overnight.

6   Make sure all the stabilizer is completely washed out of the embroidery before you lay your embroidery flat to dry; you can also put it through a tumble dryer if you are pushed for time.

7   Use small sharp scissors to carefully cut around the sheer fabric from all edges of the embroidery design, close to the outside edge row of stitching. You may also choose to use a fray block product to go around the edges of the embroidery. This stops any unraveling if you accidentally clip a thread.

8   You can also use a stencil iron (Black and Decker have just released a Dual-Temp Soldering and Craft Iron in Australia with seven interchangeable heads) to burn the cut edges of the nylon organza around the embroidery design. By doing this, no visible fabric will be seen around the edge of your embroidery.

9   You now have a freestanding embroidery design that can be applied in any position on any item, no matter what it is made of. The *Summer Wine* quilt can be made using this technique too. It would make the process slightly longer, but for some it may be easier to accomplish the embroidery placement and thus the quilt.

10   These embroidery designs can be backed with a double-sided fusible web, ironed to a quilt, garment or pillow and then free-motioned in place using monofilament thread. The decoupage embroidery pieces can also be glued to any furniture or household item (even outdoor furniture) and then treated with suitable products to ensure their protection and durability, depending on their intended usage.

11   The following projects use the *Embroidery Decoupage* technique, and we know that in doing them, your own *Spring Wine* creativity and imagination will be sparked.

Spring's Morn

There's nothing quite like breakfast in bed, and
there's no more perfect setting than our Spring Wine bedroom
retreat duo: a foot warmer and pillow shams.

With our lives getting busier and busier, life rushing by and the world outside ever noisier and noisier, our bedrooms are a quiet retreat we can call our own.

Taking time out for ourselves is now not so much an indulgence as a necessity – and in fact some of the most delicious hours of my life have been spent in my bedroom; it is my sanctuary.

One of my most memorable bedroom moments came one Mother's Day. My (then) teenage son Simon arrived early in the morning with a large wicker basket, announcing that he, my daughter Sam and I were going to have a 'bed picnic' breakfast. (As all my family knows, I just love breakfast in bed!) The basket was filled with all sorts of extravagant goodies – champagne (with strawberries of course), fresh orange juice, and warm croissants with jam and cream to accompany the freshly brewed coffee – all served on a white linen tablecloth on my bed … the memory is so sweet.

But you know on some days, a simple cup of tea in bed can make the day feel like a declared holiday. Taking time out like this (even if we don't have a soft-footed maid to carry our breakfast tray to and from our bedside, and we have to do it ourselves) can be just as perfect. Getting out of bed, knowing we will be getting straight back in again to sit like a princess and enjoy breakfast in bed, can be one of life's most satisfying activities.

Now it's your turn to sit back and indulge yourself. We are here to help you create the private sanctuary you deserve with our *Spring Wine* bedroom setting, so that when evening turns to night you can retire to your sleeping chamber – a private world you have created.

For those who feel that a quilt is beyond their capabilities
(for now, anyway),
this duo is the perfect way to get started
and is equally as beautiful, just like a spring morning.

Spring warmth
Foot Warmer

*A little warmth, a little light
Of love's bestowing – and so, good night!*

George Louis Palmella Busson Du Maurier

A bedroom, more than any other room in the house, should be an intimate retreat, and in creating it we should keep in mind that our bedrooms are rooms in which we dream; rooms where we love, heal and replenish our creative souls. In such a room we can be most comfortable with ourselves; these rooms are sanctuaries, where we can satisfy and challenge our deepest needs – they are rooms of sheer delight.

Note: Check the size of your bed (ours was made for a queen size) and change the measurement for the white waffle-weave fabric (the center of the foot warmer) accordingly.

Materials

- Bernina Arista 730E sewing machine and embroidery module
- Oval embroidery hoop (145mm x 255mm)
- Bernina embroidery software Version 5 and transfer device
- Summer Wine design CD (included free with this book)
- 2½yd x 60in white waffle-weave fabric
- 2yd x 45in lime green gingham for borders and appliqué
- 2½yd x 45in white cotton fabric to back foot warmer
- Small piece of double-sided fusible web to back appliqué fabric and Embroidery Decoupage
- One, 5yd x 60in bolt of Jenny's Quilt Magic lightweight fusible batting (you will need the length for the foot warmer and this should be enough for the pillow shams as well)
- Small piece of sheer fabric for decoupage (enough for four hoopings)
- Four white tassels for the corners of the foot warmer
- Machine feet: embroidery foot/darning foot No 26, ¼in patchwork foot No 37 and open-toe appliqué foot No 20
- Machine needle: Jeans size 80
- Bernina Gold Latched bobbin case (this comes with the machine) for embroidery
- Threads: Robison-Anton rayon 40 embroidery threads in the following colors: Light Pink (No 2243), Pink (No 2223), Rose Tint (No 2591), Wild Pink (No 2259), Bone (No 2582), Cottage Beige (No 2593), Pistachio (No 2250) and Snow White (No 2297)
- Bobbinfil, 80 weight, to wind Bernina bobbins
- Bernina metal bobbins
- White construction thread for needle and bobbins
- Sulky polyester transparent thread
- Dissolve Magic woven soluble stabilizer for Embroidery Decoupage
- Water-soluble fabric-marking pen
- Rotary cutter, self-healing cutting mat and quilting ruler
- Small sharp scissors to cut out appliqué
- Glass-headed quilting pins
- Spray bottle for water to remove placement marks
- Good surge of steam iron
- Hand-sewing needle
- General sewing requirements

PREPARATION

1   Use the rotary cutter, self-healing cutting mat and quilting ruler to cut the following:

from the waffle-weave fabric and the *Quilt Magic* lightweight fusible batting:

—one, 18in x 85in rectangle for the foot warmer

from the lime green gingham and the *Quilt Magic* lightweight fusible batting:

—3½in bias strips joined on the bias to measure 7yd for the borders

from the white cotton fabric:

—one, 22½in x 90½in rectangle for the backing.

2   Use a hot, clean (remember we are working on white fabric) steam iron to fuse the lightweight fusible batting to the back of all matching fabric pieces. The batting will have to be ironed (in 3½in x 60in wide strips) to the back of the 7yd bias border strip, butting up the ends so that no joins are apparent from the right side of the fabric.

3   Use the quilting ruler and fabric-marking pen to mark a 4½in diagonal grid on the 18in x 85in waffle-weave rectangle backed with fusible batting. Start by marking in the two diagonal lines that will intersect at the center of the fabric, then measure out 4½in from these lines. This way the marked grid remains centered in the fabric rectangle.

4   Iron the double-sided fusible web on the back of four small pieces of lime green gingham; this will be used in the *Embroidered Decoupage*.

5   Refer to pages 58–59 to create the *Embroidered Decoupage*. You will be using design **sw19** and you will need four of these designs, two mirrored. This technique also uses the Bernina embroidery software and transfer device, the *Summer Wine* design CD, Robison-Anton embroidery threads in a Jeans 80 needle, the embroidery foot and embroidery hoop, the Gold Latched bobbin, soluble stabilizer, small sharp scissors, metal bobbins filled with bobbinfil, a small piece of sheer fabric and the lime green gingham backed with double-sided fusible web.

6   Iron the double-sided fusible web to the back of the four **sw19** embroidery designs, again referring to pages 58–59 where we explain how to do this the easy way.

QUILTING

7   Use the white construction thread in the needle and bobbin, the open-toe appliqué foot and a straight stitch to quilt the 4½in marked diagonal grid on the white waffle-weave rectangle backed with fusible batting.

8   Use the spray bottle filled with water to generously spray the quilted foot warmer, then lie it flat to dry naturally.

9   Use the rotary cutter, self-healing cutting mat and quilting ruler to square up the quilted waffle-weave rectangle, maintaining the quilted grid centered to 16½in x 84½in.

CONSTRUCTION

10   Use the ¼in patchwork foot and white construction thread in the needle and bobbin to attach the 3½in bias-cut lime green gingham borders to the four sides of the quilted foot warmer.

11   Attach the 3½in bias-cut lime green gingham borders backed with fusible batting to the edge of the 16½in x 84½in quilted waffle-weave rectangle, mitering the corners (in your preferred method) as you go.

EMBROIDERED DECOUPAGE

12   Use the photo as a guide to position the **sw19** decoupage designs centered on the foot warmer, mirroring when necessary, then use a hot steam iron to fuse them in place.

13   Adjust the height of the pressure foot to easily clear the loft of the quilting and the embroidered decoupage designs, then use the freehand embroidery foot and the transparent thread to sew the embroidery designs to the quilted top using a small stipple stitch that sews on and off the embroidery design.

14   Continue the construction using the ¼in patchwork foot to attach the 22½in x 90½in backing fabric to the foot warmer, leaving a 12in opening for turning. Remember to pin a tassel in each corner of the warmer. The tassel should face to the center of the footwarmer, pinned to the right side of the fabric, making sure the tassel cord extends past the raw fabric edge in the corners. The tassel will then be attached when the backing fabric is sewn to the back of the foot warmer.

15   Turn the foot warmer to the right side, making sure the corners are pushed all the way out, and then press both the back and front of the foot warmer, turning under a small hem on the opening and pinning it with glass-headed pins. Use a hand-sewing needle and thread to sew the turning opening closed.

16   Use white thread in the needle and bobbin to stitch-in-the-ditch through both the foot warmer top and the backing in the seam line around the center foot warmer rectangle (where the bias lime green gingham borders are attached to the foot warmer front).

17   Press the foot warmer and put it at the bottom of your bed.

When we're in bed, comfort comes first,
and warm feet are a must for a good night's sleep.
So curl up under the covers knowing that your 'tootsies'
are nice and snug under your foot warmer –
this wonderful feeling was described by George Eliot:
I wish the sky would rain down roses …
it would be like sleeping and yet waking all at once.

Pillows
to Dream on

71

*On a wet Sunday, when you waken to the gentle patter of rain
against the window and the world seems at peace,
think of it as a gift, an opportunity to snuggle back down on your pillows.*

*In the softness of pillows
we can find comfort,
renewed optimism
and strength
— a total revival of spirit.*

Note: Check the size of your
actual pillows and change the
measurement for the white waffle-weave
fabric (the center of the pillow sham)
accordingly.

PREPARATION

1   Use the rotary cutter, self-healing cutting mat and quilting ruler to cut the following:

from the waffle-weave fabric and the *Quilt Magic* lightweight fusible batting:

—two, 22in x 29in rectangles for the pillow shams

from the lime green gingham and the *Quilt Magic* lightweight fusible batting:

—3½in bias strips joined on the bias to measure 9yd for the pillow sham borders

from the white cotton fabric:

—four, 24in x 26in rectangles for backing the pillow shams.

Materials

- Bernina *Arista 730E* sewing machine and embroidery module
- Oval embroidery hoop (145mm x 255mm)
- Bernina embroidery software *Version 5* and transfer device
- *Summer Wine* design CD (included free with this book)
- ⅔yd x 60in white waffle-weave fabric for pillow shams
- 2yd x 45in lime green gingham for borders and appliqué
- 2yd x 45in white cotton fabric to back pillow shams
- Small piece of double-sided fusible web to back appliqué fabric and *Embroidery Decoupage*
- One, 5yd x 60in bolt of Jenny's *Quilt Magic* lightweight fusible batting (a 1yd bolt is not enough for the two pillow shams, but this should be enough for the foot warmer also)
- Small piece of sheer fabric for decoupage (enough for two hoopings)
- Machine feet: embroidery foot/darning foot No 26, ¼in patchwork foot No 37 and open-toe appliqué foot No 20
- Machine needle: Jeans size 80
- Bernina *Gold Latched* bobbin case (this comes with the machine) for embroidery
- Threads: Robison-Anton rayon 40 embroidery threads in the following colors: Light Pink (No 2243), Pink (No 2223), Rose Tint (No 2591), Wild Pink (No 2259), Bone (No 2582), Cottage Beige (No 2593), Pistachio (No 2250) and Snow White (No 2297)
- Bobbinfil, 80 weight, to wind Bernina bobbins
- Bernina metal bobbins
- White construction thread for needle and bobbins
- Sulky polyester transparent thread
- *Dissolve Magic* woven soluble stabilizer for *Embroidery Decoupage*
- Water-soluble fabric-marking pen
- Rotary cutter, self-healing cutting mat and quilting ruler
- Small sharp scissors to cut out appliqué
- Glass-headed quilting pins
- Spray bottle for water to remove placement marks
- Good surge of steam iron
- General sewing requirements

2　Use a hot, clean (remember we are working on white fabric) steam iron to fuse the lightweight fusible batting to the back of all matching fabric pieces. The batting will have to be ironed (in $3\frac{1}{2}$in x 60in wide strips) to the back of the 9yd bias border strip, butting up the ends so that no joins are apparent from the right side of the fabric.

3　Use the quilting ruler and fabric-marking pen to mark a $4\frac{1}{2}$in diagonal grid on each 22in x 29in waffle-weave rectangle backed with fusible batting. Start by marking in the two diagonal lines that will intersect at the center of the fabric, then measure out $4\frac{1}{2}$in from these lines. This way the marked grid remains centered in the fabric rectangle.

4　Iron the double-sided fusible web on the back of two small pieces of lime green gingham; this will be used in the *Embroidered Decoupage*.

5　Refer to pages 58–59 to create the *Embroidered Decoupage*. You will be using design **sw19** and you will need two of these designs, one mirrored vertically. This technique also uses the Bernina embroidery software and transfer device, the *Summer Wine* design CD, embroidery threads in a Jeans 80 needle, the embroidery foot and embroidery hoop, soluble stabilizer, small sharp scissors, metal bobbins filled with bobbinfil, the small piece of sheer fabric (enough for two hoopings) and the lime green gingham backed with double-sided fusible web.

6　Iron the double-sided fusible web to the back of the two **sw19** embroidery designs, again referring to pages 58–59 where we explain how to do this the easy way.

QUILTING

7　Use the white construction thread in the needle and bobbin, the open-toe appliqué foot and a straight stitch to quilt the $4\frac{1}{2}$in marked diagonal grid on both of the white waffle-weave rectangles backed with fusible batting.

8　Use the spray bottle filled with water to generously spray both quilted pillow shams, then lie them flat to dry naturally.

9　Use the rotary cutter, self-healing cutting mat and quilting ruler to square up the quilted waffle-weave rectangles, maintaining the quilted grid centered to 20in x $27\frac{3}{4}$in.

CONSTRUCTION

10　Use the $\frac{1}{4}$in patchwork foot and white construction thread in the needle and bobbin to attach the $3\frac{1}{2}$in bias-cut lime green gingham borders to the four sides of each pillow sham.

11　Attach the $3\frac{1}{2}$in bias-cut lime green gingham borders backed with fusible batting to the edge of the 20in x $27\frac{3}{4}$in quilted waffle-weave rectangles, mitering the corners (in your preferred method) as you go.

EMBROIDERED DECOUPAGE

12　Use the photo as a guide to position the **sw19** decoupage design on each pillow sham, then use a hot steam iron to fuse them in place – and remember that one of the designs is mirrored when you position them in opposite corners of the shams.

13　Adjust the height of the pressure foot to easily clear the loft of the quilt and the embroidered decoupage designs, then use the freehand embroidery foot and the transparent thread to sew the embroidery designs to the quilt top using a small stipple stitch that sews on and off the embroidery design.

14　Continue the construction using the open-toe foot to turn under a double 1in hem on the 26in side of both of the white cotton backing rectangles.

15　Continue the pillow construction by overlapping the two hemmed fabric pieces. The wrong side of the top piece should be facing the right side of the underneath fabric, with the hemmed edges facing the outside edge of the pillow and the overlapped fabric pieces forming a 26in x $33\frac{3}{4}$in rectangle. Use the glass-headed pins to pin down the overlaps along the raw fabric edges, then stitch them together with a narrow hem along the raw fabric overlap edge only.

16　Place the overlapped pillow sham backing fabric over the pillow sham front, right sides together, then pin around the edges and sew around all four sides.

17　Turn the pillow sham to the right side, making sure the corners are pushed all the way out, and then press both the pillow sham front and back.

18　Use white thread in the needle and bobbin to stitch-in-the-ditch through both the pillow sham top and the backing in the seam line around the center pillow sham rectangle (where the bias lime green gingham borders are attached to the pillow sham front).

19　Press the pillow shams and insert your pillows.

Now you have created pillow shams with fabrics as soft as a mother's caress, and mementoes that are meaningful to you as you continue on your journey of accomplishment and self-discovery.

Days of
wine and roses
Mirror

A mirror fit for a princess!
This timeless treasure would grace
any bedroom or bathroom,
carrying the Spring Wine theme
from the garden into the house
using the Embroidered
Decoupage technique.

B eauty is in the eyes of the beholder, we are told. But without even looking into the mirror we can imagine how a *Spring Wine* embroidery could turn a blank folk art piece into a beautiful collector's item.

HOW EASY IS IT?

1   Remove the mirror and its backing from the frame.

2   Paint the blank mirror frame with several coats of an off-white acrylic paint, sanding between coats.

3   Edge the outer rim of the mirror frame with narrow piping made from a striped green fabric that has been cut on the bias. Glue this around the edge of the mirror frame so that the piping sits just above the edge of the frame. Cut the raw fabric edge of the bias piping short of the back side of the edge of the frame, and then glue a ½in flat braid over the top to cover it.

4   Place the mirror back into the frame and the backing onto the mirror.

5   Use the photo as a guide when you glue the embroidery on your mirror, and don't be afraid to cut sections from another embroidery, applying it as an extension of a design (just as you would for fabric appliqué or decoupage).

6   You may choose to remove the clip from the back of a butterfly brooch and glue it at the top of the mirror frame.

7   When the glue is dry, paint PVA glue over the embroidery – this seals it and protects it from dust and mould.

This mirror goes perfectly with our Spring Wine pillow shams and bed warmer, to complete the bedroom setting.

Mirror, mirror on the wall,
who's the
fairest of them all?

Spring wine is usually pink, sparkling, light and refreshing, and so too is this enchanting pillow set.
Using the same design as we used in the Summer Wine pillow, we again show what a difference fabric and thread colors can make.

Spring Wine Pillows

We decided to continue this spring theme of soft pinks and lime green to create the Spring Wine pillow duo. Below are the instructions for the pink check-edged pillow; simply substitute fabrics for the green gingham-edged pillow.

PREPARATION

1   Use the self-healing cutting mat, quilting ruler and rotary cutter to cut the following:

from the white linen and *Quilt Magic* lightweight fusible batting:

—one, 12in square for pillow top

from the pink checked fabric and *Quilt Magic* lightweight fusible batting:

—two, 3in x 12in strips for top and bottom of pillow

—two, 3in x 17in strips for sides of pillow

from the pink checked fabric only:

—one, 12in x 17in strip for backing fabric

—one, 8in x 17in strip for backing fabric.

2   Use a hot steam iron to press the batting to the back of the matching sized fabric pieces; also fuse the double-sided fusible web to the back of the lime green gingham fabric to be used for the appliqué.

3   Stabilize the white linen 12in square with several coats of heavy-duty spray starch, ironing between coats.

4   Use the fabric-marking pen and quilting ruler to mark vertical and horizontal lines that intersect at the center of the white linen 12in square. (This is a good way to test your fabric-marking pen, to make sure it can be removed with water once the pillow is complete.)

5   Wind two Bernina bobbins with Bobbinfil.

Materials

- Bernina *Arista 730E* sewing machine and embroidery module
- Oval embroidery hoop (145mm x 255mm)
- Bernina embroidery software *Version 5* and transfer device
- *Summer Wine* design CD (included free with this book)
- One 12in square of white linen for center of pillow
- 24in x 45in strip of soft pink checked fabric for borders and backing
- Small piece of lime green gingham fabric for appliqué
- Small piece of double-sided fusible web to back appliqué fabric
- 1¾yd soft pink and green tied tassel edging braid
- One 12in pillow insert
- 1yd x 60in bolt of *Quilt Magic*, lightweight fusible batting
- Machine feet: embroidery foot/darning foot No 26, *BSR* (Bernina Stitch Regulator) (these two feet come with the machine), ¼in patchwork foot No 37 and open-toe appliqué foot No 20
- Machine needles: Jeans size 80 and 120 wing needle
- Bernina *Gold Latched* bobbin case (this comes with the machine) for embroidery
- Threads: Robison-Anton rayon 40 embroidery threads in the following colors: Light Pink (No 2243), Pink (No 2223), Rose Tint (No 2591), Wild Pink (No 2259), Bone (No 2582), Cottage Beige (No 2593), Pistachio (No 2250) and Snow White (No 2297)
- Bobbinfil, 80 weight, to wind Bernina bobbins
- Bernina metal bobbins
- White construction thread for needle and bobbins
- *Hoop Magic*, Jenny's self-adhesive tear-away stabilizer for embroidery backing
- Heavy-duty spray starch
- Water-soluble fabric-marking pen
- Rotary cutter, self-healing cutting mat and quilting ruler
- Small sharp scissors to cut out appliqué
- Glass-headed quilting pins
- Spray bottle for water to remove placement marks
- Good surge of steam iron
- General sewing requirements

EMBROIDERY

Use the embroidery foot, the Gold Latched bobbin case, a Jeans 80 needle threaded with Robison-Anton rayon 40 embroidery thread, the Bernina bobbin wound with Bobbinfil and *Hoop Magic* sticky stabilizer in the oval embroidery hoop.

6   Refer to pages 10–14 to download the basting stitch from the Bernina website to place around the embroidery design.

7   Use the Bernina software and transfer device to transfer design **sw19** with the basting stitch around it from the *Summer Wine* design CD (included with this book) to the machine.

8   Embroider design **sw19** centered on the white linen 12in square backed with fusible batting, using the lime green gingham fabric for the appliqué.

9   The following are the thread stops and color sequence for **sw19**:

⊘   **Color 1**   Snow White (No 2297)   Scroll outline
Place the lime green gingham fabric backed with double-sided fusible web over the design outline.

⊘   **Color 2**   Snow White (No 2297)   Scroll outline
Remove the hoop from the machine (not the fabric from the hoop), then use small sharp scissors to carefully cut out the appliqué fabric close to and parallel to the row of stitching. Place the hoop back in the machine.

⊘	Color 3	Pistachio (No 2250)	Appliqué stitch
⊘	Color 4	Snow White (No 2297)	Appliqué stitch
⊘	Color 5	Cottage Beige (No 2593)	Small leaves
⊘	Color 6	Bone (No 2582)	Stem
⊘	Color 7	Pistachio (No 2250)	Large leaves
⊘	Color 8	Wild Pink (No 2259)	Flower petals
⊘	Color 9	Rose Tint (No 2591)	Shading petals
⊘	Color 10	Pink (No 2223)	Front petals
⊘	Color 11	Light Pink (No 2243)	Shading front petals
⊘	Color 12	Snow White (No 2297)	Flower center
⊘	Color 13	Pink (No 2223)	Turn-back petal
⊘	Color 14	Bone (No 2582)	Leaf veins

10   Remove the hoop from the machine, then clip the basting stitches and all the jump threads. Carefully tear the stabilizer from the fabric, removing as much stabilizer as possible from the back of the embroidery.

Press the embroidery from the front.

11   Use water in the spray bottle to remove the pen marks from your work. Allow it to dry naturally, then press it again from the front.

QUILTING

12   You may choose to use the Bernina Stitch Regulator (BSR) to quilt in and around the embroidery on the white linen 12in square, using a small stipple stitch.

CONSTRUCTION

13   Use construction thread in the needle and bobbin and the ¼in patchwork foot to construct the pillow.

14   Take the two 17in-wide pink checked fabric pieces, and turn under a 1in hem on the 17in side of each piece.

15   Join the two, 3in x 12in strips to the top and bottom of the white linen 12in square, and then the two, 3in x 17in strips to the sides.

16   Press all seams to the side of the pink checked fabric.

HEM STITCHING

17   Use the open-toe appliqué foot, the 120 wing needle, white construction thread and a hem stitch (width and length 3.0) to sew around the edge of the center linen square.

18   Start with the needle in the white linen fabric. The stitch then swings over the pink checked fabric (and the seam at the back) and back into the original hole, punched by the wing needle. Keep your eye on the needle, ensuring it remains at all times in the white linen fabric and aligned with and parallel to the edge of the pink checked fabric. Sew around all four sides of the center linen square.

19   Continue the pillow construction by overlapping the two hemmed pink checked fabric pieces. The wrong side of the top piece should be facing the right side of the underneath fabric, with the hemmed edges facing the outside edge of the pillow and the overlapped fabric pieces forming a 17in square. Use the glass-headed pins to pin down the overlaps along the raw fabric edges, then stitch them together with a narrow hem along the raw fabric overlap edge only.

20   Place the overlapped pillow backing fabric over the pillow front, right sides together, then pin around the edges and sew around all four sides.

21   Turn the pillow to the right side, making sure the corners are pushed all the way out, and then press both the pillow front and back.

22   Use white thread in the needle and bobbin to stitch-in-the-ditch through both the pillow top and the backing in the seam line around the center pillow square (where the pink checked borders are attached to the pillow front).

23   Attach the 1¾yd soft pink and green tied tassel edging braid to the front of the pillow around the outside edge of the pink checked borders.

24   Place the 12in insert in the pillow.

Repeat for the second pillow, eliminating the braid and using green gingham for the borders.

*How did you enjoy your first sips
of Spring Wine?
These pillows would grace any
reclining lounge or swing chair
on a sunlit porch or gazebo,
along with the table and chairs in
the following projects.*

Spring Wine
Throw

This Spring Wine chair or bed throw
celebrates the launch of a brand new range
of exciting quilting designs called
Pride and Plumage,
created by our own Kim Bradley.

*Kim, as we all know, is an accomplished long-arm quilter
who is now venturing out into her own designs
for long-arm computerized quilting along with design CDs
for the domestic range of embroidery machines.*

These glorious continuous quilting designs are taken from a whole-cloth quilt design for the long-arm quilting machine, and broken down in size to suit a domestic sewing machine. Kim has had a wonderful time experimenting with designs on her Bernina *Artista 730E* and Bernina embroidery software Version 5.

Materials

- Bernina *Artista 730E* sewing machine and embroidery module
- Oval embroidery hoop (145mm x 255mm)
- Bernina embroidery software *Version 5* and transfer device
- *Summer Wine* design CD (included free with this book) and *Pride and Plumage* quilting design CD by Kim Bradley
- 1yd x 45in white fabric for throw top and backing
- 2½yd x 45in soft pink checked fabric for borders and binding
- 14in x 9in piece of sheer light-colored fabric (such as cotton tulle or nylon organza) for embroidery decoupage
- Small piece of lime green gingham fabric for appliqué
- Small piece of double-sided fusible web to back appliqué fabric and embroidery design
- 1yd x 60in bolt of *Quilt Magic* lightweight fusible batting
- Machine feet: embroidery foot/darning foot No 26, *BSR* (Bernina Stitch Regulator) No 42, open-toe appliqué foot No 20 and ¼in patchwork foot No 37
- Machine needles: Jeans size 80 and 120 wing needle
- Bernina *Gold Latched* bobbin case (this comes with the machine) for embroidery
- Threads: Robison-Anton rayon 40 embroidery threads in the following colors: Light Pink (No 2243), Pink (No 2223), Rose Tint (No 2591), Wild Pink (No 2259), Bone (No 2582), Cottage Beige (No 2593), Pistachio (No 2250) and Snow White (No 2297)
- Bobbinfil, 80 weight, to wind Bernina bobbins
- White cotton 80 weight thread for stipple quilting and pink cotton thread for embroidered quilting designs
- Sulky polyester transparent thread for embroidery decoupage
- Bernina metal bobbins wound with Bobbinfil
- White construction thread for needle and bobbins
- *Dissolve Magic*, Jenny's woven soluble stabilizer (two layers used for each hooping)
- Rotary cutter, self-healing cutting mat and quilting ruler
- Vellum tracing paper to print templates
- Awl to punch placement holes in templates
- Water-fading fabric-marking pen
- Basting spray
- Small sharp scissors
- Good surge of steam iron
- One page of photocopy paper or similar
- Sticky tape
- Hand-sewing needle and thread
- General sewing requirements

PREPARATION

1   Turn to *Embroidery Decoupage* on pages 58–59 and embroider two **sw19** designs (one mirrored vertically) following the directions on those pages. Use the lime green gingham fabric backed with double-sided fusible web for the appliqué, the sheer fabric, Gold Latched bobbin case, metal bobbins wound with Bobbinfil, woven soluble stabilizer, Jeans 80 needle, embroidery foot, embroidery hoop, Bernina embroidery software and transfer device and the threads listed in materials list for your embroidery.

2   Place the photocopy paper on the ironing board with the two **sw19** designs on top, right side down (the stabilizer should be washed out and the designs cut out and ironed). Now put a piece of double-sided fusible web that is the same size as the paper on top of the designs (the web side is facing the wrong side of the designs). Fuse the web to the back of the embroidery designs; the excess web will stick to the paper.

3   When the designs have cooled, remove the web paper from the embroidery designs (they will have attached to the photocopy paper with the web), pull the designs from the photocopy paper, remove the excess web from in and around the embroidery designs and place the two designs to one side.

4   Use the Bernina embroidery software and transfer device and a PC to transfer designs **250E1** (shell), **250D1** (urn), **250D2** (heart-shaped leaves), **250C3** (long feathers and scrolls), **250C1** (part one of plumes) and **250C2** (part two of plumes) from the *Pride and Plumage* design CD to the sewing machine and print templates for all designs.

5   Use the awl to punch placement holes in the center and on each side of the center on the vertical and horizontal divide lines.

6   Refer to the picture of the throw to combine the following design templates, and then hold them together with sticky tape:

250D1

250D2

—designs **250D1** and **250D2** to make the urn and leaves

250C1

250C2

—designs **250C1** and **250C2** to make half the long feather design.

7   Use the rotary cutter, self-healing cutting mat and quilting ruler to cut the following:

from the white fabric:

—two, 36in squares for the throw top and backing

from the soft pink checked fabric and the lightweight fusible batting:

—four, 4in x 29½in strips for the top and bottom borders of the throw (top and backing)

—four, 4in x 37in strips for the side borders of the throw (top and backing)

—2½in bias strips, joined on the bias to measure 5yd for the throw binding

from the lightweight fusible batting:

—one, 36in square to back the center of the throw

—two, 4in x 29½in strips to back the top and bottom borders of the throw

—two, 4in x 37in strips to back the side borders of the throw.

8   Use a hot steam iron to fuse the batting to the back of the white 36in square for the center of the throw, and the 4in soft pink checked fabric strips for the borders.

9   Use the quilting ruler and fabric-making pen to mark vertical, horizontal and diagonal lines that intersect at the center of the white 36in square for the center of the throw.

10   Measure out and mark on the white 36in square backed with fusible batting:

—14½in from the center on the four diagonal lines; this is the center of the urn and leaves combination template for designs **250C1** and **250C2**

—9½in on each side of the center on the horizontal divide line; this position marks the base of the 'shell' quilting design **250E1**

—2in on each side of the horizontal divide line, then use the quilting ruler to mark a line that passes through this point and is parallel to the marked horizontal divide line. This line is used to position the continuous long feather designs made up of designs **250C1** and **250C2**.

11   Use the quilt basting spray to hold the 36in square of backing fabric to the back of the batting on the white 36in throw center. Use a well ventilated area for spraying and follow the manufacturer's directions.

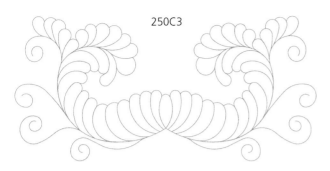

250C3

The white 36in square, batting and basted backing fabric are used for all quilting designs.

12   Use the embroidery foot, pink thread in the Jeans 80 needle, the oval embroidery hoop and a bobbin wound with white thread to embroider all the quilting designs.

13   All three 36in square layers of fabric for the throw (white marked fabric for the top, batting and white backing fabric) are hooped together when embroidering the quilting designs.

14   Use the single or combination placement templates and fabric-marking pen to mark the positions for the quilting designs (see the *Summer Wine* quilt on pages 10–14 for more information on the use of templates). These are embroidered in the following sequence (refer to the picture of the quilt):

—combination design for the continuous feathers (**250C1** and **250C2**) this is embroidered on each side of the center horizontal line so that each half of the design starts at the intersection of the line marked 2in in line (parallel to the horizontal divide line). Remember to flip the combination template for these designs horizontally to mark the placement positions for the opposite half of the combination design

—design **250C3** centered under the combination feather designs

—shell design **250E1** on each side of the center, on the horizontal divide line, so the bottom of the shell design sits over the 9^1/$_2$in marked position

—combination urn and leaves designs **250D1** and **250D2** centered over the 14^1/$_2$in marked position on the diagonal lines; the urn faces the center of the square.

15   When all the embroidery is complete, clip any jump threads and press your work.

FREEHAND QUILTING

16   Use the 80 weight white thread in the Jeans 80 needle and the BSR foot to stipple-quilt in and around the embroidered feather quilt designs, starting from the center and working to the edge of the white 36in square.

EMBROIDERY DECOUPAGE

17   Use the photo as a guide to placing the two **sw19** embroidered decoupage designs, and when you are happy with the positions of the designs, iron them in place using a hot steam iron.

18   Adjust the height of the pressure foot to easily clear the loft of the throw and the embroidered decoupage designs. Next, use the freehand embroidery foot and the transparent thread to sew the embroidery designs to the throw top, using a small stipple stitch that sews on and off the embroidery design.

19   Square the center of the throw to 29^1/$_2$in.

CONSTRUCTION

20   Use construction thread in the Jeans 80 needle and bobbin and the ^{1}/$_4$in patchwork foot to attach the borders to the throw.

21   The border and backing fabric pieces are attached in the one seam:

—from the back of the center quilted square, the right side of the pink checked border backing fabric is placed right side to the throw with the raw edges of the backing fabric aligned

—from the front of the center quilted square, the right side of the pink checked border fabric (backed with fusible batting) is placed to the right side of the quilted square, with the raw fabric edges aligned

—vertically pin all fabric layers together and then stitch them together in one seam

—from the right side of the throw, press the border strips flat

—from the wrong side of the throw, use the basting spray on the batting (on the wrong side of the border fabric piece), then press the border backing fabric over the batting and press it.

22   Attach the borders to the throw in the following sequence:

—4in x 29½in pink checked fabric strips (top and backing) to the top and bottom of the throw.

Press the top and bottom borders and the backing to the back of the borders before attaching the:

—4in x 37in pink checked fabric strips (top and backing) to the sides of the throw.

Press the side borders and the backing to the back of the side borders.

HEM STITCHING

23   Use the white construction thread in the 120 wing needle, construction thread in the bobbin and the open-toe foot to sew a hem stitch around the outside edge of the center of the throw.

24   Select a hemstitch (width 4, length 3), so the needle starts in the white fabric and swings over the pink border fabric (and sandwiched seam). As you sew the straight stitch the needle should, at all times, be on the white fabric, and the straight stitch should align with the seam of the pink fabric with the needle swinging into the pink border fabric. Sew around all four sides of the white center square.

25   Sign and date your throw. See page 55 in the construction of the *Summer Wine* quilt for the French binding technique instructions.

This fresh little throw is a perfect way to learn how to use Kim's fabulous new quilting designs, taken from her Pride and Plumage design CD — and you have a lovely project to show for it at the end!

A throw such as this is ideal on the back of a cane chair or over a chaise longue, and it looks equally as beautiful on a table as it is both decorative and functional.

Thank you Kim for sharing these great new designs with us. For more information on Kim's quilting design CDs, including *Pride and Plumage* (for both domestic and long-arm computerized machines) or for her custom quilting, contact Kim on phone: 61 2 9659 2912, email her on: kbr35115@bigpond.net.au or visit her website: www.kimbradleycreations.com to see more of her wonderful quilts and for information on her classes.

Enchanted
Garden Setting

*How fitting is this enchanting garden setting
for our Spring Wine Embroidered Decoupage concept!*

We have transformed relatively inexpensive tin chairs and a table into a provincial garden setting, reminiscent of those glorious outdoor pieces you may have seen on a sunlit garden patio in a Tuscan villa. Using the *Embroidered Decoupage* technique described on pages 58–59, design sw19 is applied to the tin garden setting. It is just perfect for showing off your *Spring Wine* pillows, and of course serving your *Spring Wine* on!

Refer to pages 58-59 for the instructions on how to create *Embroidered Decoupage* designs. You will need five sw19 designs (one of which is mirrored vertically).

We have used craft glue to glue the embroidery designs to the back of each chair and three on the table. Refer to the photo as a guide when you start.

When the glue is completely dry (allow at least 24 hours), you will need to treat the top of the table and the backs of the chairs with a weather-resistant sealant such as a clear outdoor varnish. This will protect the embroidery from extremes of weather and make it waterproof. If you choose to leave the furniture inside or undercover, simply paint the embroidery with PVA glue (available from any hardware store). This is white when applied but it dries clear. Once it is dry the embroidery will be like plastic, and so it will be protected from dust and mildew. It can also be easily cleaned – simply wipe it with a damp sponge. Note, however, that this does not make your embroidery weather-proof and so it is unsuitable for an outdoor setting.

Perhaps if you close your eyes, imagine you are Shirley Valentine as you sip your wine, with the sun setting over the Mediterranean and waves gently lapping around your ankles, you can truly savor the moment of your *Spring Wine* – bellissima!

Spring Wine
Recipe

Sangria is a spring/summer wine punch, originating in Spain.
Its light, fruity and slightly bubbly taste
is just perfect for long summer lunches, picnics at the beach
or a dusk concert in the park. So good is this recipe for sangria
that you will probably want to make double.

INGREDIENTS

One bottle of red wine (Cabernet Sauvignon, Merlot, Rioja, Zinfandel or Shiraz)

One lemon, cut into wedges

One orange, cut into wedges

One lime, cut into wedges

Two tablespoons of sugar

Splash of orange juice

Two shots of gin

One cup of sliced strawberries or raspberries (fresh or frozen)

One small can of diced pineapple (with juice)

Four cups of ginger ale

Ice

PREPARATION

Pour the wine into a pitcher and then squeeze the juice from the orange, lemon and lime wedges into the wine. Toss the wedges (minus the seeds) in as well, along with the pineapple, sugar, orange juice and gin.
Chill overnight and then add ginger ale, berries and ice. Sangria can be made and served immediately, using chilled wine and served over lots of ice, but the best sangria is chilled for about 24 hours in the refrigerator before it is consumed, allowing the flavors to really marinate.

Sangria – perfect for sipping at your
Spring Wine table as you recline on your
Spring Wine pillow!

Embroidery designs, thread stops and color sequence

The 20 designs on the *Summer Wine* design CD are listed by name (**sw01** to **sw20**) with their thread stops and color sequence. Refer to these at all times as you embroider each section of the quilt and the individual designs that make up a combination design.

> ### TIP *from the Winemaker*:
> Should you choose to use any of the alternative colors suggested on pages 16–19.
> Make a note of your thread colors and numbers on the list below. This will make it easier
> when you are stitching out the designs. Remember, the first and second colors (usually Colors 1 and 2)
> of each appliqué fabric design or design sequence should be as close to the color of the fabric
> selected for the appliqué as possible.

Design sw01: Appliqué design only

Color 1   Black (No 2296)   Scroll outline
Place the black fabric backed with double-sided fusible web over the design outline.

Color 2   Black (No 2296)   Scroll outline
Remove the hoop from the machine (not the fabric from the hoop), then use small sharp scissors to carefully cut out the appliqué fabric close to and parallel to the row of stitching. Place the hoop back in the machine.

Color 3   Metallic Gold (No 1003)   Appliqué stitch
Color 4   TH Burgundy (No 2608)   Appliqué stitch

Design sw02

Design sw01

Design sw02:
Appliqué design only

Color 1   Black (No 2296)   Scroll outline
Place the black fabric backed with double-sided fusible web over the design outline.

Color 2   Black (No 2296)   Scroll outline
Remove the hoop from the machine (not the fabric from the hoop), then use small sharp scissors to carefully cut out the appliqué fabric close to and parallel to the row of stitching. Place the hoop back in the machine.

Color 3   Metallic Gold (No 1003)   Appliqué stitch
Color 4   TH Burgundy (No 2608)   Appliqué stitch

Design sw03

Color 1   Black (No 2296)   Scroll outline

Place the black fabric backed with double-sided fusible web over the design outline.

Color 2   Black (No 2296)   Scroll outline

Remove the hoop from the machine (not the fabric from the hoop), then use small sharp scissors to carefully cut out the appliqué fabric close to and parallel to the row of stitching. Place the hoop back in the machine.

Color 3   Metallic Gold (No 1003)   Appliqué stitch

Color 4   TH Burgundy (No 2608)   Appliqué stitch

Design sw03: Embroidery and appliqué design

Color 1   Golden Tan (No 2570)   Leaf stem

Color 2   Black (No 2296)   Scroll outline

Place the black fabric backed with double-sided fusible web over the design outline.

Color 3   Black (No 2296)   Scroll outline

Remove the hoop from the machine (not the fabric from the hoop), then use small sharp scissors to carefully cut out the appliqué fabric close to and parallel to the row of stitching. Place the hoop back in the machine.

Color 4   Metallic Gold (No 1003)   Appliqué stitch

Color 5   Olive Drab (No 2317)   Leaf

Color 6   Golden Tan (No 2570)   Leaf veins

Design sw05

Design sw04

Design sw04:
Embroidery design only

Color 1	Olive Drab (No 2317)	Small leaves		Color 5	Warm Wine (No 2496)	Back petal
Color 2	Golden Tan (No 2570)	Stem		Color 6	TH Burgundy (No 2608)	Shading back petal
Color 3	Pistachio (No 2250)	Large leaves		Color 7	Passion Rose (No 2499)	Front petal
Color 4	Golden Tan (No 2570)	Veins		Color 8	Salmon (No 2299)	Shading front petal

Design sw06

Design sw06: Embroidery design only

Color 1	Olive Drab (No 2317)	Small leaves
Color 2	Golden Tan (No 2570)	Stem
Color 3	Pistachio (No 2250)	Large leaves
Color 4	Golden Tan (No 2570)	Veins
Color 5	Warm Wine (No 2496)	Back petal
Color 6	TH Burgundy (No 2608)	Shading back petals
Color 7	Passion Rose (No 2499)	Front petal
Color 8	Salmon (No 2299)	Shading front petals
Color 9	Metallic Gold (No 1003)	Flower center
Color 10	Passion Rose (No 2499)	Turn-back petal

Design sw08: Embroidery design only

Color 1	Olive Drab (No 2317)	Small leaves
Color 2	Golden Tan (No 2570)	Stem
Color 3	Pistachio (No 2250)	Large leaves
Color 4	Golden Tan (No 2570)	Veins
Color 5	Warm Wine (No 2496)	Back petals
Color 6	TH Burgundy (No 2608)	Shading back petals
Color 7	Passion Rose (No 2499)	Front petals
Color 8	Salmon (No 2299)	Shading front petals
Color 9	Metallic Gold (No 1003)	Flower center
Color 10	Passion Rose (No 2499)	Turn-back petal

Design sw07

Design sw08

Design sw07: Embroidery design only

Color 1	Olive Drab (No 2317)	Small leaves
Color 2	Golden Tan (No 2570)	Stem
Color 3	Pistachio (No 2250)	Large leaves
Color 4	Golden Tan (No 2570)	Veins
Color 5	Warm Wine (No 2496)	Back petals
Color 6	TH Burgundy (No 2608)	Shading back petals
Color 7	Passion Rose (No 2499)	Front petals
Color 8	Salmon (No 2299)	Shading front petals
Color 9	Metallic Gold (No 1003)	Flower center
Color 10	Passion Rose (No 2499)	Turn-back petal

Design sw09

Design sw09: Appliqué design only

| Color 1 | Black (No 2296) | Scroll outline |

Place the black fabric backed with double-sided fusible web over the design outline.

| Color 2 | Black (No 2296) | Scroll outline |

Remove the hoop from the machine (not the fabric from the hoop), then use small sharp scissors to carefully cut out the appliqué fabric close to and parallel to the row of stitching. Place the hoop back in the machine.

| Color 3 | TH Burgundy (No 2608) | Appliqué stitch |
| Color 4 | Metallic Gold (No 1003) | Appliqué stitch |

Design sw11: Embroidery and appliqué design

Color 1	Metallic Gold (No 1003)	Grid
Color 2	Golden Tan (No 2570)	Stem
Color 3	Black (No 2296)	Scroll outline

Place the black fabric backed with double-sided fusible web over the design outline.

| Color 4 | Black (No 2296) | Scroll outline |

Remove the hoop from the machine (not the fabric from the hoop), then use small sharp scissors to carefully cut out the appliqué fabric close to and parallel to the row of stitching. Place the hoop back in the machine.

| Color 5 | Black (No 2296) | Scroll outline |

Place the black fabric backed with double-sided fusible web over the design outline.

| Color 6 | Black (No 2296) | Scroll outline |

Remove the hoop from the machine (not the fabric from the hoop), then use small sharp scissors to carefully cut out the appliqué fabric close to and parallel to the row of stitching. Place the hoop back in the machine.

Design sw10: Embroidery design only

Design sw10

Color 1	Olive Drab (No 2317)	Small leaves
Color 2	Golden Tan (No 2570)	Stem
Color 3	Pistachio (No 2250)	Large leaves
Color 4	Golden Tan (No 2570)	Veins
Color 5	Olive Drab (No 2317)	Turn-backs on leaves

Design sw11

Color 7	Metallic Gold (No 1003)	Appliqué stitch
Color 8	TH Burgundy (No 2608)	Appliqué stitch
Color 9	Pistachio (No 2250)	Leaves
Color 10	Golden Tan (No 2570)	Veins

Design sw12

Design sw13

Design sw12: Embroidery design only

Color 1	Olive Drab (No 2317)	Small leaves
Color 2	Golden Tan (No 2570)	Stem
Color 3	Pistachio (No 2250)	Large leaves
Color 4	Golden Tan (No 2570)	Veins
Color 5	Warm Wine (No 2496)	Back petals
Color 6	TH Burgundy (No 2608)	Shading back petals
Color 7	Passion Rose (No 2499)	Front petals
Color 8	Salmon (No 2299)	Shading front petals
Color 9	Metallic Gold (No 1003)	Flower center
Color 10	Passion Rose (No 2499)	Turn-back petal

Design sw14

Design sw13: Embroidery and appliqué design

Color 1	Olive Drab (No 2317)	Small leaves
Color 2	Golden Tan (No 2570)	Stem
Color 3	Passion Rose (No 2499)	Back petal
Color 4	Salmon (No 2299)	Front petal
Color 5	Black (No 2296)	Scroll outline

Place the black fabric backed with double-sided fusible web over the design outline.

| Color 6 | Black (No 2296) | Scroll outline |

Remove the hoop from the machine (not the fabric from the hoop), then use small sharp scissors to carefully cut out the appliqué fabric close to and parallel to the row of stitching. Place the hoop back in the machine.

| Color 7 | Metallic Gold (No 1003) | Appliqué stitch |
| Color 8 | TH Burgundy (No 2608) | Appliqué stitch |

Design sw14: Embroidery design only

Color 1	Olive Drab (No 2317)	Small leaves
Color 2	Golden Tan (No 2570)	Stem
Color 3	Pistachio (No 2250)	Large leaves
Color 4	Golden Tan (No 2570)	Veins
Color 5	Olive Drab (No 2317)	Turn-backs on leaves
Color 6	Passion Rose (No 2499)	Front petals
Color 7	Salmon (No 2299)	Shading front petals

Design sw15

Design sw15: Embroidery design only

Color 1	Olive Drab (No 2317)	Small leaves
Color 2	Golden Tan (No 2570)	Stem
Color 3	Warm Wine (No 2496)	Petals
Color 4	TH Burgundy (No 2608)	Shading on petals
Color 5	Metallic Gold (No 1003)	Center of flower

Design sw17: Embroidery design only

Color 1	Olive Drab (No 2317)	Small leaves
Color 2	Golden Tan (No 2570)	Stem
Color 3	Pistachio (No 2250)	Large leaves
Color 4	Golden Tan (No 2570)	Veins
Color 5	Warm Wine (No 2496)	Back petals
Color 6	TH Burgundy (No 2608)	Shading back petals
Color 7	Passion Rose (No 2499)	Front petals
Color 8	Salmon (No 2299)	Shading front petals
Color 9	Metallic Gold (No 1003)	Flower center
Color 10	Passion Rose (No 2499)	Turn-back petal

Design sw16

Design sw17

Design sw16: Embroidery design only

Color 1	Olive Drab (No 2317)	Small leaves
Color 2	Golden Tan (No 2570)	Stem
Color 3	Pistachio (No 2250)	Large leaves
Color 4	Golden Tan (No 2570)	Veins
Color 5	Olive Drab (No 2317)	Turn-backs on leaves

Design sw18

Design sw18: Appliqué design only

Color 1	Black (No 2296)	Scroll outline

Place the black fabric backed with double-sided fusible web over the design outline.

Color 2	Black (No 2296)	Scroll outline

Remove the hoop from the machine (not the fabric from the hoop), then use small sharp scissors to carefully cut out the appliqué fabric close to and parallel to the row of stitching. Place the hoop back in the machine.

Color 3	Metallic Gold (No 1003)	Appliqué stitch
Color 4	TH Burgundy (No 2608)	Appliqué stitch

Design sw19: Appliqué design only

Color 1	Black (No 2296)	Scroll outline

Place the black fabric backed with double-sided fusible web over the design outline.

Color 2	Black (No 2296)	Scroll outline

Remove the hoop from the machine (not the fabric from the hoop), then use small sharp scissors to carefully cut out the appliqué fabric close to and parallel to the row of stitching. Place the hoop back in the machine.

Color 3	Metallic Gold (No 1003)	Appliqué stitch
Color 4	TH Burgundy (No 2608)	Appliqué stitch
Color 5	Olive Drab (No 2317)	Small leaves
Color 6	Golden Tan (No 2570)	Stem
Color 7	Pistachio (No 2250)	Large leaves
Color 8	Warm Wine (No 2496)	Back petals
Color 9	TH Burgundy (No 2608)	Shading back petals
Color 10	Passion Rose (No 2499)	Petals
Color 11	Salmon (No 2299)	Shading front petals
Color 12	Metallic Gold (No 1003)	Flower center
Color 13	Passion Rose (No 2499)	Turn-back petal
Color 14	Golden Tan (No 2570)	Stem

Design sw19

Design sw20

Design sw20: Embroidery design only

Color 1	Olive Drab (No 2317)	Small leaves
Color 2	Golden Tan (No 2570)	Stem
Color 3	Passion Rose (No 2499)	Back petals
Color 4	Salmon (No 2299)	Front petal

Charge your glasses
and drink a toast to...

Nothing just happens on its own – there is always a cast of (what often seems like) thousands behind any venture, and Jenny and Simon would like to ask you to raise your glasses and thank the talented team that supports them and has helped make this book happen (once again) almost overnight.

Editor:
Jenny Haskins
Quilt by:
Jenny and Simon Haskins

Publisher: Thanks to Simon Blackall and Diane Wallis, the talented duo from The Watermark Press who have been with us from the start back in 1999, and who always know what to do when it comes to publishing, and then do it with class. Thank you for being part of *Summer Wine*.

Designer: Suzy King of Suzy King Design is the magic designer behind Jenny's and Simon's books and magazines. Her special flair and ability to get inside Jenny's head and improve on it is a rare gift indeed – perhaps she could market this!

Subeditor: Nina Paine is able to take what is written and edit it in such a way that it is clear and to the point, yet retains Jenny's warm and fuzzy 'voice', making it a pleasure to read. (It also makes the author look really good!) Thank you Nina, you are a true professional.

Photographer: Tom Evangelidis, photographer extraordinaire! Tom captures the mood, color and style in every shot, thus making anything he photographs look better than the real thing. Keep him warm and well-fed and Tom can turn out magic photography with classic charm and style that reflects his Greek ancestry.

Stylist: Robyn Wilson (with a little help from Jenny). What do we say about you Robbie – your warmth, friendship and creative talent endear you to all who cross your path, and your talent as a stylist is reflected in every picture Tom takes. Added to that, you are part of this book in so many other ways – making projects, keeping Jenny calm and just being you – thank you for keeping us all on track and being so very special.

Barbara Sunderlage, a relatively new face to Quilters' Resource, instigated this *Summer Wine* book. She had seen the quilt in the office and immediately sent me an email asking when the book would come out – how was that for positive thinking? Barbara has fast become a friend and colleague of Jenny's and Simon's, and working with her is a privilege as her professional integrity is reflected in everything she does. Barbara, we look forward to working with you and Quilters' Resource for many years to come, and we thank you for your support.

Kevin Anderson and Kerrie Hay of Bernina Australia are two of the most generous, giving and supporting people in the sewing industry in Australia, as well as being friends and colleagues. Nothing is ever too much trouble and Jenny and Simon could not have done this book without their support and friendship.

Gayle Hillert of Bernina USA, whose gentle ways and giving spirit touch all who come in contact with her; we love working with you Gayle.

Martin Favre, the President of Bernina USA, is a leading force in the sewing industry in America, with his passion and drive for excellence. Thank your Martin for your support with the wonderful Bernina products, and for your belief in us.

Andreea Sparhawk of Robison-Anton threads, who is responsible for Jenny and Simon using glorious RA threads in this book and all their projects. The success of any project is dependant on color and design, and RA lights up the life of any project with shimmering colors that reflect the personality of the artist and confirm the quality and range of RA threads to all who use them.

Ricky and Kay Brooks, from RNK Inc. for the wonderful Quilt Magic batting, Hoop Magic self-adhesive tear-away stabilizer and the Dissolve Magic woven soluble stabilizer, all distributed by them under the Jenny Haskins' Private Collection range. Thank you for your support of products and promotion, not to mention your friendship. Ricky has me doing things before I have even thought of them and as for Simon doing things – well he has a skiing holiday with Ricky (and Kay) – how like a man!

John Upton, my partner and 'mate' – thank you for your gentle ways and for being so patient with me, supporting me during the endless hours I spend at my computer (till the wee small hours of the morning). Thank you too for the countless cups of tea, for taking over the household duties after a hard day's physical work, for pretending to understand my sewing terms, and for gazing adoringly at the endless stream of photos I show you, saying 'They are beautiful darling!' What would Mz Honey and I do without you?

Now is the time to relax in your enchanted garden, lean back on your SpringWine pillow to enjoy the sweetness of your SummerWine quilt – savor the bouquet and color of your special vintage and enjoy the reviews.

Who knows where Jenny and Simon will take you on your next venture into their world of machine-embroidered quilts!

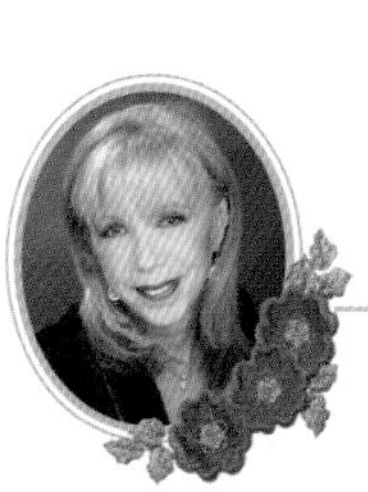

The Jenny Haskins *Design Collection*

Showing the way to your creative jorney

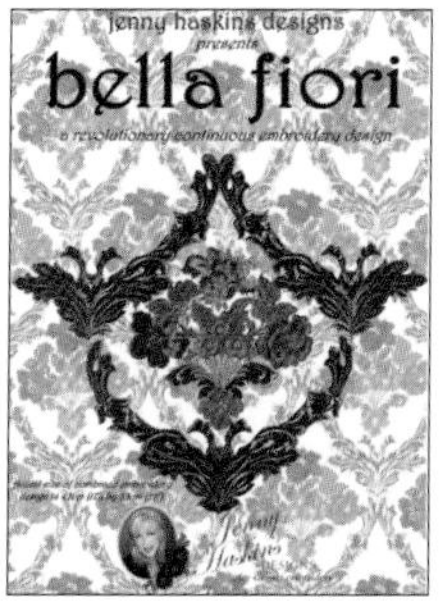
jenny haskins designs
presents
bella fiori

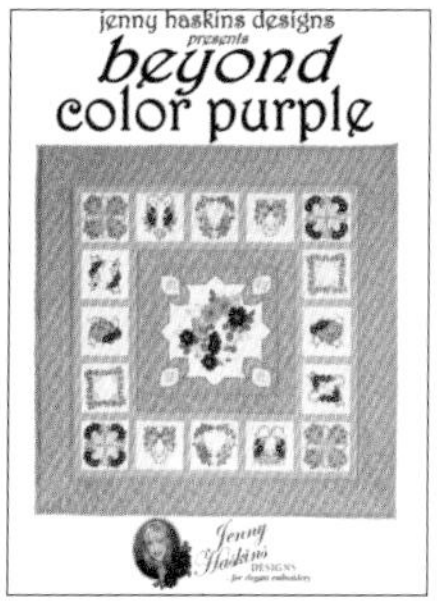
jenny haskins designs
presents
beyond
color purple

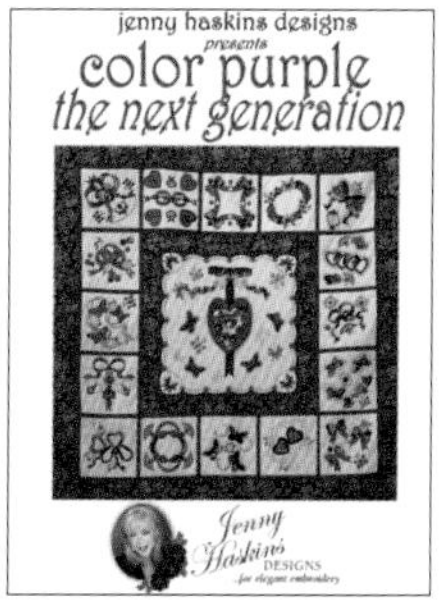
jenny haskins designs
presents
color purple
the next generation

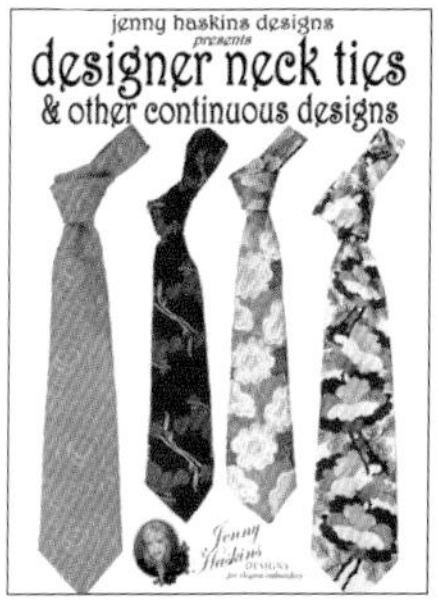
jenny haskins designs
designer neck ties
& other continuous designs

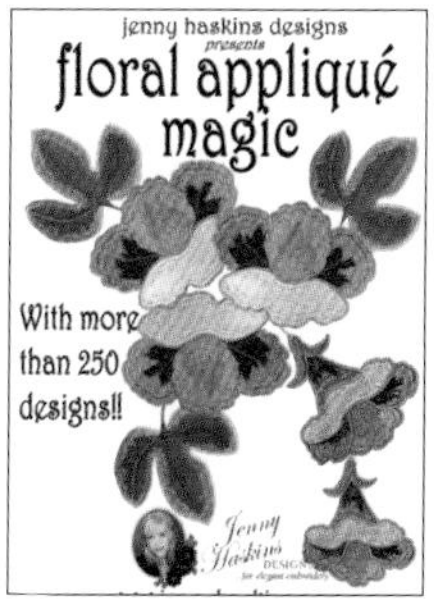
jenny haskins designs
presents
floral appliqué
magic
With more than 250 designs!!

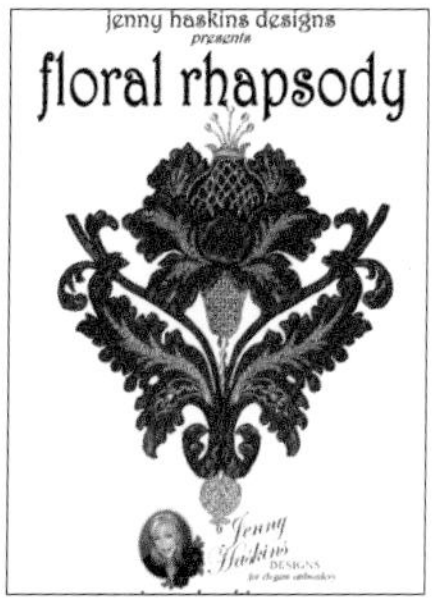
jenny haskins designs
presents
floral rhapsody

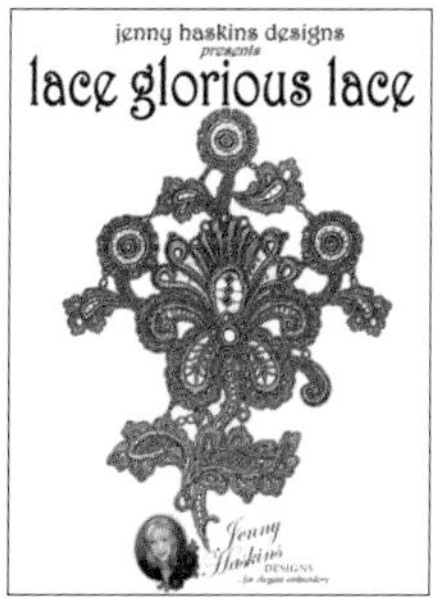
jenny haskins designs
presents
lace glorious lace

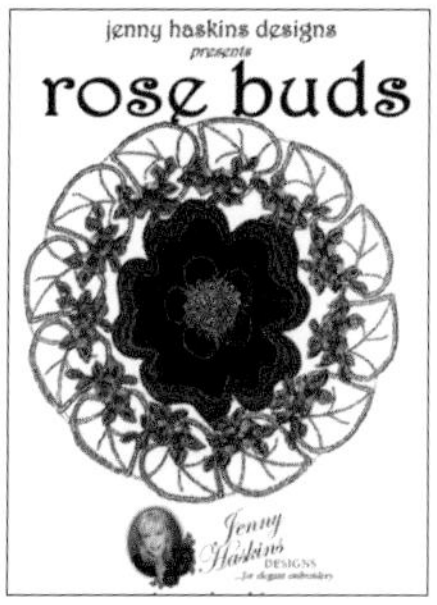
jenny haskins designs
presents
rose buds

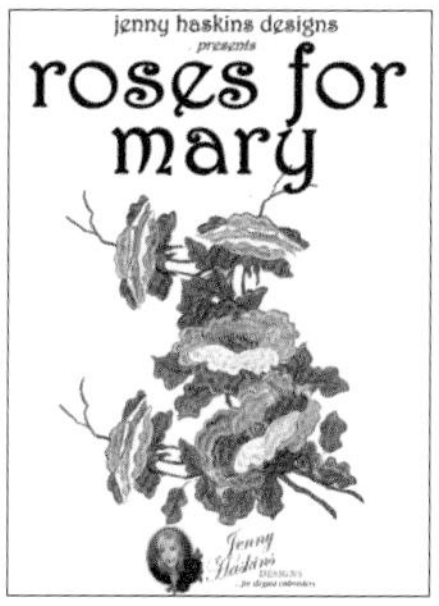
jenny haskins designs
presents
roses for
mary

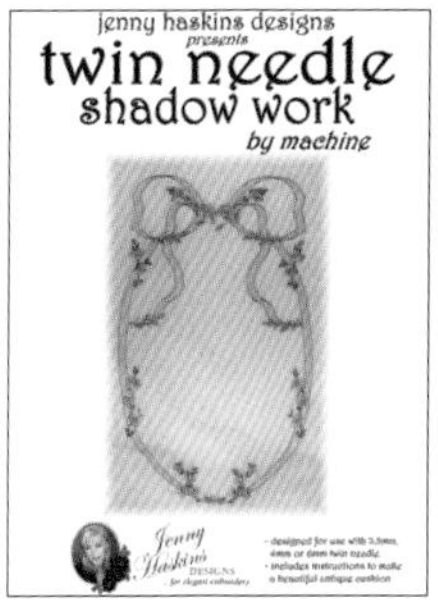
jenny haskins designs
presents
twin needle
shadow work
by machine

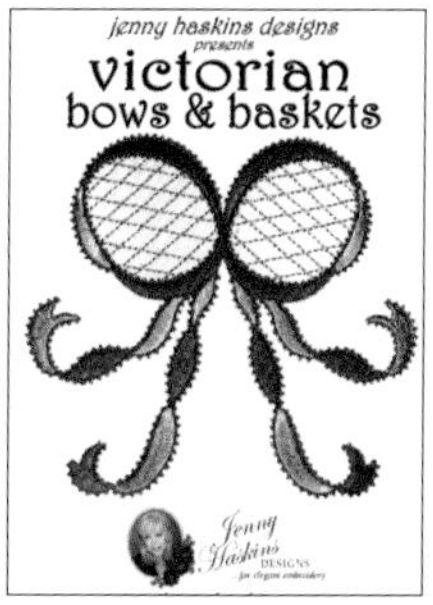
jenny haskins designs
presents
victorian
bows & baskets

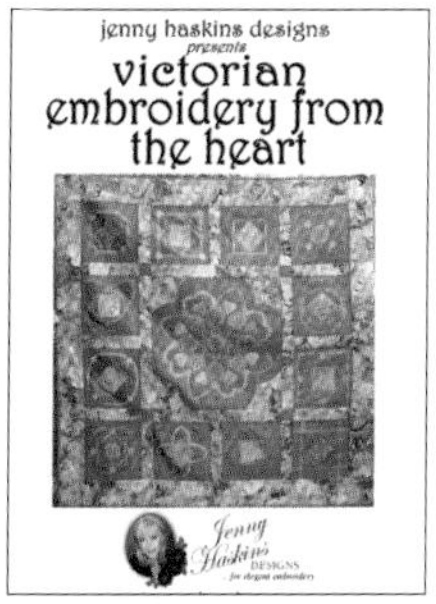
jenny haskins designs
presents
victorian
embroidery from
the heart

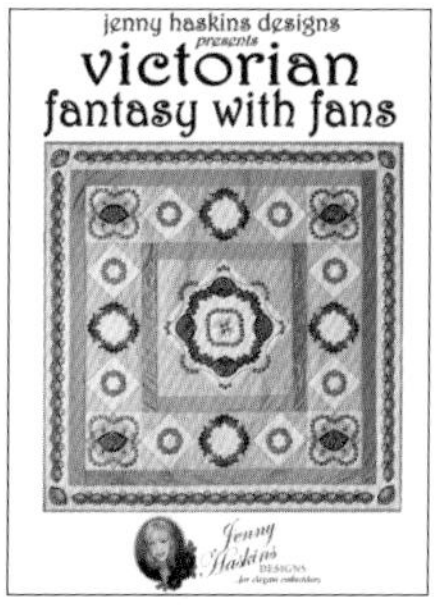
jenny haskins designs
presents
victorian
fantasy with fans

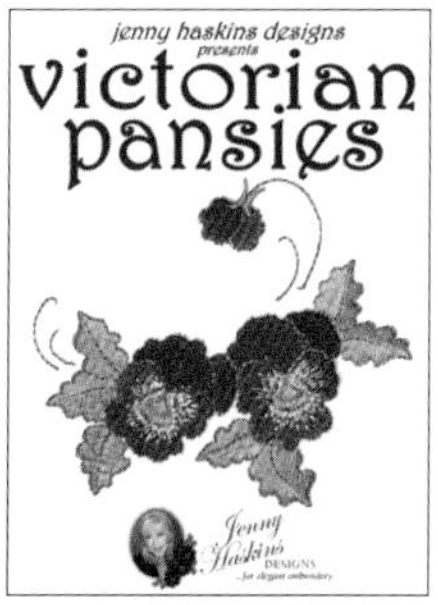
jenny haskins designs
presents
victorian
pansies

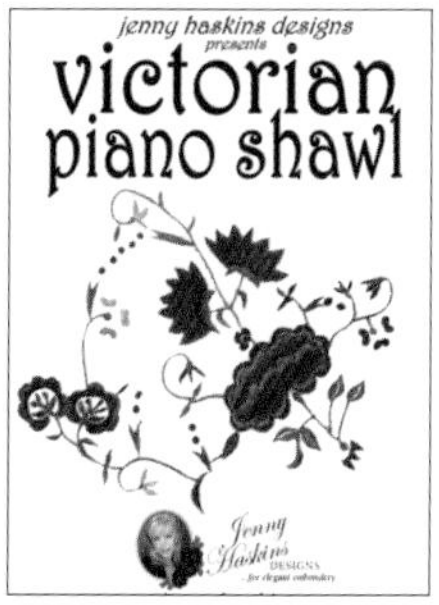
jenny haskins designs
presents
victorian
piano shawl

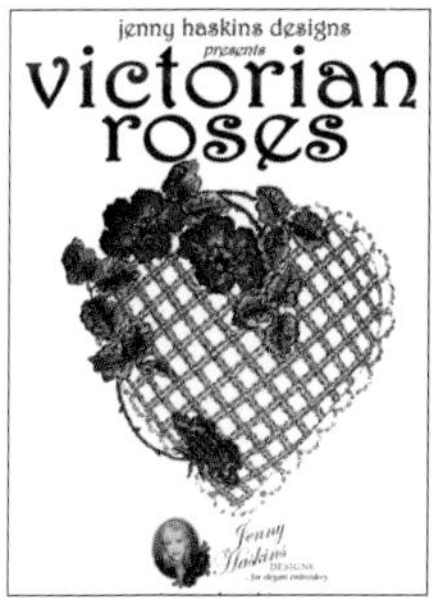
jenny haskins designs
presents
victorian
roses

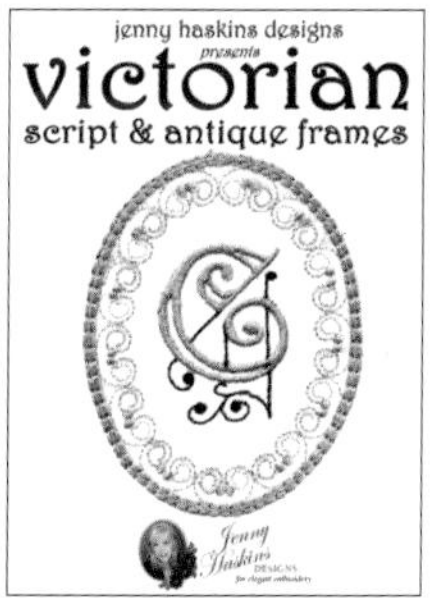
jenny haskins designs
presents
victorian
script & antique frames

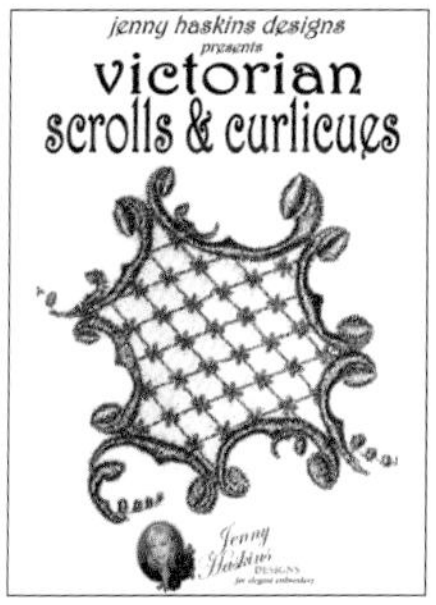
jenny haskins designs
presents
victorian
scrolls & curlicues

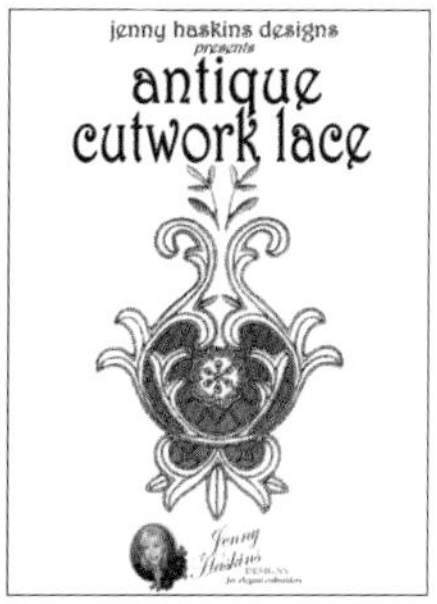
jenny haskins designs
presents
antique
cutwork lace

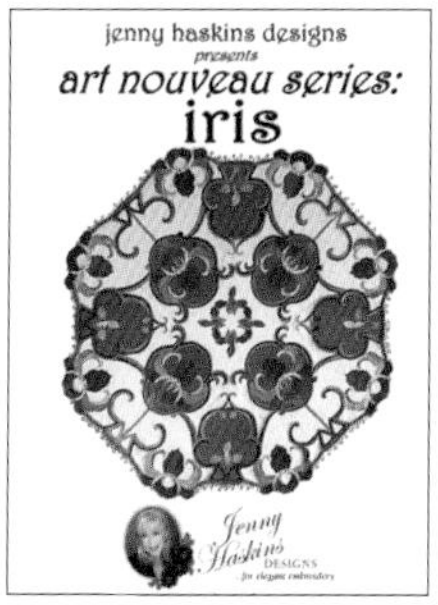
jenny haskins designs
presents
art nouveau series:
iris

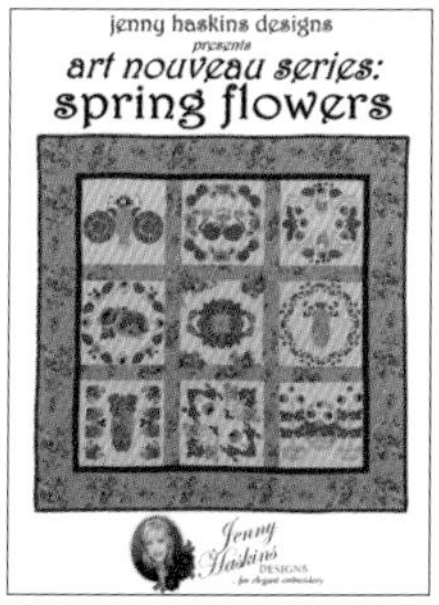
jenny haskins designs
presents
art nouveau series:
spring flowers

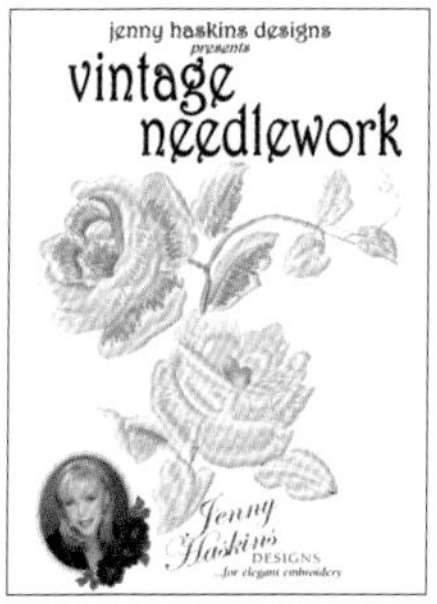
jenny haskins designs
presents
vintage
needlework

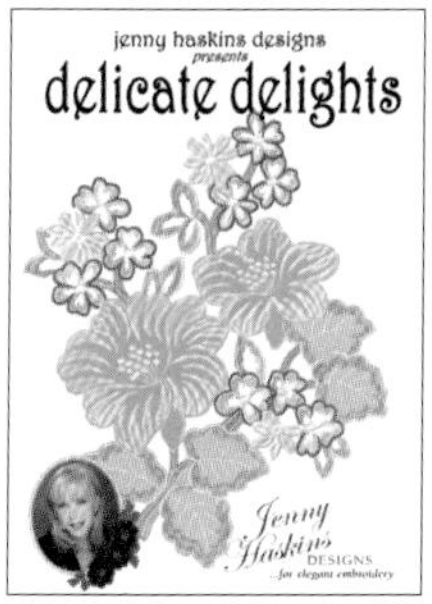
jenny haskins designs
presents
delicate delights

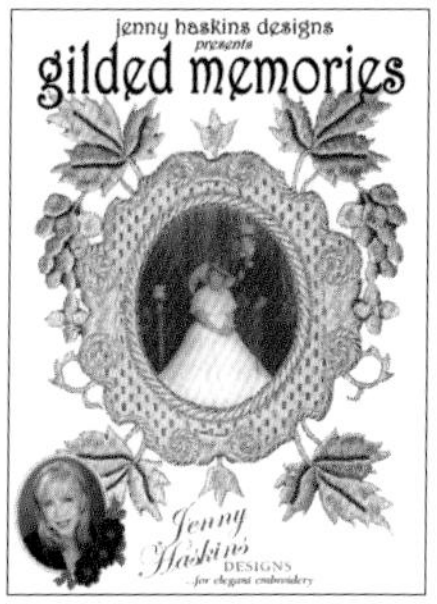
jenny haskins designs
presents
gilded memories

available from:

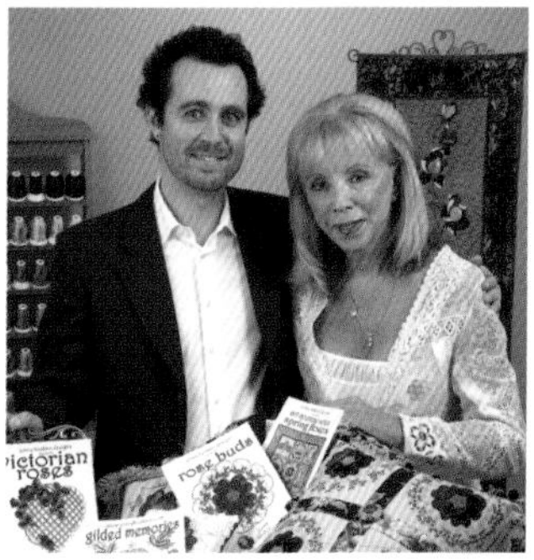

Unique Creative Opportunities (Aust)
Phone +61 2 9680 1381
Fax +61 2 9680 1381
Email jenny@rpi.net.au
www.jennyhaskins.com

Quilters' Resource (US)
Phone 1800 676 6543
www.quiltersresource.com

Books by
Jenny Haskins

Victorian Dreams	Sally Milner Publishing
Color Purple	(sold out) see *Creative Expressions* No 12 & No 13 for directions
The Federation Quilt	(sold out) see *Creative Expressions* No 15 to send for directions on a similar quilt
Amadeus	Aussie Publishing
Inspirational Machine Embroidered Quilting (Arsenic and Old Lace quilt)	Aussie Publising
Victorian Pansies	Quilters' Resource (sold out)
Victorian Roses	Quilters' Resource (sold out)
Victorian Splendor	Quilters' Resource (sold out)
Inspirational Home Décor	Brother Australia (sold out)
Latte Quilt with Kerrie Hay	Quilters' Resource
Roses for Mary	Quilters' Resource
MarJen for Error	Creative Living Media
Simon's Folly	Creative Living Media
Spectacular Fashion	Creative Living Media
Moulin Rouge	Creative Living Media
Creative Expressions Magazine	Creative Living Media
Aquamarine Ambience	Quilters' Resource
Summer Wine	Quilters' Resource